English Lexical Semantics

ALSO AVAILABLE FROM BLOOMSBURY

Morphology in English: Word Formation in Cognitive Grammar, Zeki Hamawand
Semantics, Kate Kearns
Applying Cognitive Linguistics in the English Language Classroom, Benjamin White and Natalia Dolgova

English Lexical Semantics

A Cognitive Linguistics Approach

ZEKI HAMAWAND

BLOOMSBURY ACADEMIC
LONDON • NEW YORK • OXFORD • NEW DELHI • SYDNEY

BLOOMSBURY ACADEMIC
Bloomsbury Publishing Plc, 50 Bedford Square, London, WC1B 3DP, UK
Bloomsbury Publishing Inc, 1385 Broadway, New York, NY 10018, USA
Bloomsbury Publishing Ireland, 29 Earlsfort Terrace, Dublin 2, D02 AY28, Ireland

BLOOMSBURY, BLOOMSBURY ACADEMIC and the Diana logo are
trademarks of Bloomsbury Publishing Plc

First published in Great Britain 2025

Copyright © Zeki Hamawand, 2025

Zeki Hamawand has asserted his right under the Copyright, Designs and
Patents Act, 1988, to be identified as Author of this work.

For legal purposes the Acknowledgements on p. ix constitute an
extension of this copyright page.

Cover design: Jade Barnett
Cover image © Pawel Czerwinski/Unsplash

All rights reserved. No part of this publication may be: i) reproduced or transmitted in any form, electronic or mechanical, including photocopying, recording or by means of any information storage or retrieval system without prior permission in writing from the publishers; or ii) used or reproduced in any way for the training, development or operation of artificial intelligence (AI) technologies, including generative AI technologies. The rights holders expressly reserve this publication from the text and data mining exception as per Article 4(3) of the Digital Single Market Directive (EU) 2019/790.

Bloomsbury Publishing Plc does not have any control over, or responsibility for, any third-party websites referred to or in this book. All internet addresses given in this book were correct at the time of going to press. The author and publisher regret any inconvenience caused if addresses have changed or sites have ceased to exist, but can accept no responsibility for any such changes.

A catalogue record for this book is available from the British Library.

A catalog record for this book is available from the Library of Congress.

ISBN: HB: 978-1-3505-2046-2
       PB: 978-1-3505-2047-9
       ePDF: 978-1-3505-2043-1
       eBook: 978-1-3505-2044-8

Typeset by Integra Software Services Pvt. Ltd.
Printed and bound in Great Britain

For product safety related questions contact productsafety@bloomsbury.com.

To find out more about our authors and books visit www.bloomsbury.com
and sign up for our newsletters.

CONTENTS

Preface vii
Acknowledgements ix

PART ONE Fundamentals 1

1. Meaning 3
2. Lexical meaning 13
3. Grammatical meaning 25

PART TWO Prior approaches to lexical meaning 35

4. Traditional Lexical Semantics 39
5. Structural Lexical Semantics 51
6. Generative Lexical Semantics 73

PART THREE Cognitive Lexical Semantics 85

A Cognitive processes 97

7. The prototype theory 99
8. The frame semantics theory 109
9. The construal theory 119

B Conceptual mappings 133

10. The conceptual metaphor theory 135
11. The conceptual metonymy theory 145
12. The conceptual blending theory 153

C Usage mechanisms 161

13 The usage-based theory 163

Conclusions 173

Appendices 178
Glossary 182
Answer Key 191
Index 206

PREFACE

The present textbook provides an in-depth analysis of Lexical Semantics in English, a branch of semantics that is concerned with the study of lexical meaning. It examines the main schools of Lexical Semantics: traditional, structural, generative and cognitive. Furthermore, it emphasizes their notable contributions, important discoveries, and actual findings. Likewise, it addresses the assumptions proposed by outstanding scholars in each school, which have a profound effect on the analysis of lexical meaning. Each school adheres to a different theory of meaning. Traditional Semantics is founded on the reference and truth-conditions theories. Structural Semantics is built on the theories of lexical fields and lexical relations. Generative Semantics is based on Componential Analysis, Natural Semantic Metalanguage and Conceptual Semantics. Cognitive Semantics, which is the most recent trend, hinges on the theories of prototype, frame semantics, and construal and conceptual associations such as metaphor, metonymy and blending. The purpose of the study is to show that cognitive theories have descriptive and explanatory power to explain lexical meaning.

Approach

The approach adopted is Cognitive Lexical Semantics, a subpart of Cognitive Semantics that focuses on the relationship between meaning and the mind. The primary concern is how the mind processes language in relation to meaning, analysing meaning in terms of mental operations that aid in producing and understanding linguistic expressions. Language is deployed as a lens through which mental operations can be observed. Lexical items are studied as reflections of operations such as categorization, configuration and conceptualization. Similarly, meaning is examined in terms of conceptual structures that help conceptualize experiences and shape linguistic expressions. Lexical items are seen as reflections of structures like metaphor, metonymy and blending. The meanings of lexical items are understood as related to concepts in the minds of language users rather than to objects in the external world. Meaning is considered encyclopaedic, with lexical items serving as entry points to vast repositories of knowledge about a given linguistic concept. Language itself does not encode meaning; instead, lexical items serve as prompts or act as cues for constructing meaning.

Objectives

The textbook explores Lexical Semantics, detailing how the meaning of a lexical item is determined. To achieve this, the investigation connects theory with practice, with two main objectives. The theoretical objective is to clarify the meaning of a lexical item and how it is defined. In this context, it familiarizes students with the theories of lexical meaning, introduces key concepts used in the study of meaning and elaborates on essential principles proposed for analysing semantic structure effectively. The practical objective is to acquaint students with the methods for analysing semantic structures and inform them about techniques for explaining their interpretations. The ultimate goal is to demonstrate that the methods employed by Cognitive Lexical Semantics for examining meaning are highly valuable, with the strategies they propose being crucial. To fulfil its purpose, the textbook uses an accessible style that summarizes content through points and presents information via tables. It includes actual data, numerous examples and clear explanations.

Audiences

This textbook is aimed at two target groups. Primarily, it is intended for undergraduate students taking courses in Lexical Semantics. It provides an overview of the thinking of each linguistic school and offers comprehensive information on their assumptions, aims and methods. Additionally, it delves into the central issues involved in the study of Lexical Semantics, and teaches important areas of semantics, such as the meaning of words. Secondarily, it is aimed at students in English departments. It helps them develop their understanding of the role of meaning in human language. Precisely, it helps them to understand the meaning of lexical items and the conditions under which they are interpreted. As a guide, this textbook is targeted at two groups. First, it is aimed at linguists, focusing on the various tools used to describe semantic data. Secondly, it targets scientists in related fields, offering a description of an area in language study from different perspectives across various disciplines.

ACKNOWLEDGEMENTS

In writing this textbook, I am deeply grateful to several academics whose work has laid the foundation for the topics covered. References at the end of each chapter point to the various scholarly sources I have consulted. I also owe a debt of gratitude to many others who have not been formally acknowledged. I would like to express my appreciation to Microsoft Copilot for its assistance in drafting and refining the content of this manuscript. Its contributions significantly improved the clarity and coherence of the text. Additionally, I am thankful to the anonymous readers for their insightful comments on my work. I take full responsibility for the contents of this book. A special word of thanks goes to Sarah MacDonald, Commissioning Editor at Bloomsbury, for her exceptional editorial guidance. The team at Bloomsbury worked diligently to publish this work efficiently. Lastly, I want to thank my wife for her unwavering kindness, generosity and patience.

Zeki Hamawand

PART ONE

Fundamentals

In this part, I introduce **Lexical Semantics**, which is the branch of semantics that deals with the meanings of lexical items. Lexical items are the most noticeable components of a language. The goal is to explain the fundamental concepts underlying the study of Lexical Semantics and define them concisely. This part of the book consists of three chapters and addresses three fundamental concepts that need to be understood before delving deeply into the topic. Chapter 1 discusses the central notion of meaning, which is the characteristic of a linguistic form used to identify some aspect of the linguistic or non-linguistic world. Chapter 2 covers lexical meaning, which is the aspect of the meaning of a lexical item that is recorded in a lexicon or dictionary. Chapter 3 addresses grammatical meaning, which is the meaning contributed to the interpretation of a linguistic expression, word, clause or sentence, by the syntax of a language.

Outline

1 Meaning 3
Introduction 3
Semantics 4
Lexical Semantics 5
   Form 5
      Meaning 6
      Interpretive uncertainty 7
Lexicology 8
Summary 9
Key takeaways 9
Further reading 10
References 10

2 Lexical meaning 13
Introduction 13
Levels of lexical meaning 14
Aspects of lexical meaning 15
Types of lexical meaning 19
Summary 23
Key takeaways 23
Further reading 24
References 24

3 Grammatical meaning 25
Introduction 25
Semantic roles 26
Word order 28
Summary 33
Key takeaways 33
Further reading 34
References 34

CHAPTER ONE

Meaning

Preview

This chapter discusses the concept of meaning in language. Although meaning is complex, I aim to clarify what it entails. The goal is to explain how speakers encode meaning linguistically and how listeners decoded it. The chapter is structured as follows. The first section provides an introduction and sketches the main components of which language is composed. The second section explores the role of semantics in linguistics, dwelling on the fields of semantics and pragmatics, and drawing a comparison between the two in the study of meaning. The third section delves into Lexical Semantics, the study of word meaning, explaining the form and meaning of lexical items with a particular focus on the variability of meaning. The fourth section discusses the field of lexicology, the branch of linguistics that analyzes the lexicon of a specific language. The final section summarizes the key points of the chapter and offers some suggestions for further reading.

Introduction

Human language consists of vocal sounds or written symbols for communication. It is a complex system with distinct components, each playing a vital role. **Phonetics** studies how speech sounds are produced in a language. **Phonology** studies how speech sounds work in a language. Whereas phonetics deals with the physical properties of sounds, phonology deals with their functions. **Morphology** studies the structure of words. It analyses how prefixes and suffixes are added to form words. **Lexicology** studies the lexicon of a language. Whereas morphology studies word-forming morphemes, lexicology studies the meaning, use and behaviour of the word stock of a specific language. **Syntax** studies the structure of sentences. Whereas morphology examines how morphemes are combined to form words, syntax examines how words combine to form sentences. **Semantics** studies the meanings of words, phrases and sentences. **Pragmatics** studies the meanings of words, phrases and sentences in **context**. Whereas semantics focuses on the literal meanings of linguistic items, pragmatics focuses on their contextual use. These levels are interrelated. They work together to conduct a thorough analysis of a language. The scientific study of these language components is known as **linguistics**.

Practice 1.1

Match the following linguistic terms with their corresponding synonyms or definitions.

1. Morphology   a. word stock
2. Phonology   b. sentence structure
3. Lexicology   c. word structure
4. Semantics   d. sound function
5. Syntax   e. literal meaning

Semantics

As mentioned earlier, there are two main fields that study meaning: semantics and pragmatics. **Semantics** focuses on the context-independent meanings of linguistic expressions, defining the literal meanings that linguistic expressions carry. A linguist who specializes in this field is called a semanticist. On the other hand, **pragmatics** focuses on the context-dependent meanings of linguistic expressions, defining the non-literal meanings that linguistic expressions can have. A linguist who specializes in this field is called a pragmatist. To illustrate the difference between the two, consider the example of the sentence, *There is a car coming*. Semantically, this sentence conveys a statement that a car is approaching, without any specific context. However, pragmatically, the same sentence could be used as a warning to prevent someone from stepping onto a road at a particular moment. Semantics and pragmatics are closely related, and can be seen as two sides of the same coin. Within the field of semantics, there are two subfields of study: Lexical Semantics and Sentential Semantics. **Lexical Semantics** deals with the meanings of individual words, exploring how they are used, and how they relate to each other. **Sentential Semantics**, on the other hand, deals with the meanings of phrases and sentences, investigating how groups of words form meaningful expressions.

Lexical Semantics

As a subfield of semantics, Lexical Semantics, also known as lexico-semantics, is the study of word meanings. The word, corresponding to the term 'lexical item', is the fundamental unit of Lexical Semantics. It is the basic unit of meaning in a language. A word has two aspects. One is substance, which consists of two facets: form and meaning. The form is the orthographic representation associated with a lexical item. Meaning is the semantic content associated with a lexical item. Meaning is the characteristic of a lexical item that is used to identify some aspect of the non-linguistic world. The form serves to indicate meaning. The other aspect is use, the purpose for which a lexical item is employed. The use of a lexical item is determined by the way the language user describes a situation, which varies depending on the demands of discourse. The substance of a lexical item is activated as a response to language use. A word like *game*, for example, has two aspects that cannot be separated: the acoustic image [geɪm] and the concept 'game', referring to an activity that one engages in for amusement or fun.

Form

The form represents the concept of orthography. Words can be simple, complex or compound. A **simple word** is made up of one or more morphemes that cannot be interrupted morphologically. For example, the word *home* consists of a single lexical unit. It is a basic form that can stand alone and convey meaning. A **complex word** is made up of two or more components that can be interrupted morphologically, with one of them being a word. For instance, the word *homely* is derived from the lexical units *home* and *-ly*. A **compound word** consists of two components, both of which can be interrupted morphologically. For example, the word *homework* is a combination of the lexical units of *home* and *work*. In this study, I focus on simple words, specifically lexical items. A **lexical item** is the smallest meaningful unit of a language that can function independently or form a complete statement in speech or writing. It arises from **pairing** or linking a specific meaning with a specific form, without inflectional endings or derivational affixes, as these fall under the realm of morphology.

Practice 1.2

Underline the base that forms the smallest lexical unit in each of the following complex words.

1. unlikely
2. enlighten

3. trusteeship
4. gruesomely
5. disagreeable

Meaning

The concept of meaning refers to the semantic content attached to a word. Meaning is the conveyance of an idea or message using words in languages. The significance of a message lies in the communication between the sender and the receiver, based on the corresponding context. Two types of knowledge interact in the interpretation of a given word: lexical and encyclopaedic. They are the informational value of a word that comes into play when a word is used. Lexical knowledge is the sum of a word's linguistic properties, while encyclopaedic knowledge is the structured body of non-linguistic knowledge to which a word potentially provides access. This emphasizes the fact that the semantic content of a word is broad in scope. The meaning of a word cannot be understood independently of the vast repository of encyclopaedic knowledge to which it is linked. For example, the lexical knowledge associated with the word *pen* includes its form (pen is a count noun), its material (pen is made of plastic) and its purpose (pen is an instrument). The encyclopaedic knowledge associated with the word *pen* includes the range of actions we can do with pen (pen is used for writing, drawing, signing, playing games and bookmarking).

In connection with meaning, lexical semanticists typically address three fundamental questions:

- Do lexical items have multiple meanings, i.e. are they polysemous, and if so, on what basis are their meanings organized?
- Do lexical items occur in semantic sets, i.e. semantic frames, and if so, on what basis do they contrast with one another?
- Do two or more alternating items construe the same situation differently, and if so, on what basis are they distinguished?

Practice 1.3

What type of label each of the following statements represents in the definition of meaning?

1. The knowledge that can be expressed in a lexical item.
2. The general world knowledge surrounding a lexical item.
3. The existence of several meanings in a single lexical item.
4. The tendency of lexical items to occur in cognitive structures.
5. The choice between two rival items describing the same situation.

Finally, it is necessary to distinguish between lexical and grammatical meaning, as this is essential for understanding meaning. **Lexical meaning** refers to the definition of a word as found in a dictionary. It represents the meaning of a word considered either on its own (literal) or within a specific context (actual). This is the information that a content lexical item conveys either independently or within a sentence. **Grammatical meaning**, on the other hand, refers to the meaning of a lexical item within a grammatical context. It is the information that a word conveys within a sentence. This meaning is established once a word placed within a sentence structure, and it is the meaning that is influenced by its syntactic role. To illustrate the difference, consider the example, *The man lifted the box*. Lexically, the lexical item *man* refers to an adult male human being. Grammatically, the lexical item *man* functions as an agent or the performer of the action of lifting the box. In essence, lexical meaning is dependent on knowledge of vocabulary, while grammatical meaning is dependent on knowledge of the role of the lexical item within a sentence. In the upcoming Chapters 2 and 3, I will delve into a detailed analysis of each type of meaning.

Interpretive uncertainty

Most lexical items exhibit interpretive uncertainty in meaning, as the mapping from an expression to a meaning appears to be one-to-many rather than one-to-one. This means that one form is capable of conveying distinct meanings. Three varieties of interpretive uncertainty exist: ambiguity, vagueness and indeterminacy. They are distinct in nature and significance for semantic analysis. Uncertainty expressions are prevalent in language, arising from differences in how people understand and interpret information. They may lead to a faulty interpretation: a misinterpretation of the message made by the speaker or writer.

Ambiguity is a phenomenon whereby the form of an item has more than one meaning, and as a result, can be used to refer to different kinds of things. Ambiguity can be of two types: lexical and sentential. Lexical ambiguity arises when a lexical item can have alternative meanings. Therefore, the sentence that contains the item can be confusing because people are not sure which way to interpret it. An example is *She could not bear children*. The lexical item *bear* has an unclear meaning, as it could be understood in two ways: either 'could not give birth to children', or 'could not put up with children'. By contrast, sentential or grammatical ambiguity arises when the structure of a sentence can have alternative meanings. An example is *The host met the guest with a smile*. The prepositional phrase *with a smile* can be grouped either with the word *host* or with the word *guest*. Typically, the speaker intends just one of the alternative meanings and expects the hearer to attend to that meaning. The process of establishing a single interpretation of an ambiguous word or sentence is known as disambiguation.

Vagueness is about lack of referential clarity, resulting from giving little information about something. This occurs when the referent in the word is not clear to the hearer, meaning it cannot be stated precisely or is not sharply delimited. The meaning is imprecise enough to allow for varying interpretations. An example is *They have a house near the flow of water*. The lexical item *flow* is vague because different people might have different ideas of what a flow of water is. It is difficult to decide whether it is a brook, stream or river. A brook is smaller than a stream and a stream is smaller than a river in size. Similarly, in *She walked in an area of trees*, the phrase *an area* is vague as it is difficult to decide whether it is a grove, wood or forest. A grove is smaller than a wood and a wood is smaller than a forest in size. This is not considered lexical ambiguity because the meaning of the lexical item itself is clear; it is simply unclear which type the speaker means. It is about the under-specification of the lexical item.

Indeterminacy is about the difficulty of referent identification. This occurs when it is difficult to identify exactly, without reference to real-world knowledge, the referent of an expression. If a lexical item is indeterminate, its meaning is clear, but that meaning includes various things that the item does not distinguish between. That is, a clear border cannot be established between one thing and another. An example is *I will bring a friend*. In this sentence, there is indeterminacy in the use of the lexical item *friend*, as it could be male or female. In this case, the item is indeterminate concerning gender. Likewise, there is indeterminacy in the sentence *Alice's book is interesting*, as it could refer either to the book she wrote, or the book she bought. In this case, the item *book* is indeterminate concerning category. Such examples are not instances of lexical ambiguity because they do not require positing two distinct senses for a single lexical form. The meaning of the lexical item is clear but just does not specify what the gender or the category is.

Practice 1.4

Identify the lexical item that causes ambiguity in the sentence. Then, provide two possible meanings for each.

1. She waited near the bank.
2. The boy looks backward.
3. Jim took me to the court.
4. She broke the glasses.
5. It must be a new record.

Lexicology

The branch of linguistics that investigates the lexicon of a specific language is called lexicology. A **lexicon**, also known as lexis, is the stock of lexical items that make up a language. The lexical items are described in a book or an electronic resource called a **dictionary**. Lexicology aims to guide language users to choose the vocabulary of a language carefully. A linguist who is engaged in lexicology is known as a lexicologist. Vocabulary is tremendously important because it is the foundation of language. It is the raw building block used by humans to convey ideas, describe things, express feelings, share information, expand knowledge and improve communication. Lexicology can be approached in two ways: diachronic and synchronic. **Diachronic** or historical lexicology is devoted to the evolution of vocabulary over time. **Synchronic** or modern lexicology examines the vocabulary of a language at any given point in time, usually the present. Of the two ways, the present study is concerned with synchronic or descriptive lexicology. Lexicology is closely related to lexicography. However, they are different. Lexicology refers to the scientific study of the form, meaning and behaviour of lexical items. By contrast, lexicography refers to the art and practice of compiling, writing and editing dictionaries.

Summary

In this chapter, I have presented the foundational concepts involved in the study of Lexical Semantics. The aim was to emphasize the importance of lexical meaning. First, I introduced the branch of semantics, which is the study of meaning in language. A comparison is made between semantics and pragmatics. Semantics explains how literal meanings are linguistically encoded by speakers and decoded by hearers, while pragmatics deals with how meanings are inferred in relation to context. Secondly, I addressed Lexical Semantics, which is the subfield within semantics that studies lexical meaning in language. I highlighted the importance of a lexical item in Lexical Semantics. A lexical item is built on two axes: form and meaning. On the first axis, a lexical item is a single unit of language listed in the lexicon. On the second axis, a lexical item has its own meaning in describing a real or imaginary world. Thirdly, I presented lexicology, which specializes in analysing the lexicon of a specific language, at both diachronic and synchronic levels. A lexicon is the set of all the words in any language.

Key takeaways

- Meaning is context-dependent. The meaning of a lexical item heavily depends on the context in which it is used. Context helps determine the multiple meanings of lexical items.

- Meaning is dynamic. The meaning of a lexical item is not fixed or static. New lexical items are constantly being created, and existing lexical items can acquire new meanings.

- Meaning is subjective. Different speakers may interpret language differently based on their experiences and personal perspectives. The speaker's imprint is inherent in language.

- Meaning is communicable. The meanings of lexical items are conveyed, developed and shared within a community through social interaction and cultural practices.

- Meaning is subtle. The meanings of lexical items display slight degrees of meaning differences. Language allows for nuances, and the choice of lexical items can add layers of meaning.

Further reading

General introductions to semantics include Leech (1974), Lyons (1977, 1995), Palmer (1981), Hurford and Heasley (1983), Hoffmann (1993), Löbner (2002), Cruse (2004), Riemer (2010), Kreidler (2013), and Altshuler et al. (2019). For useful introductions to Lexical Semantics, see Cruse (1986), Pustejovsky (2006), Geeraerts (2015), Goddard and Wierzbicka (2013), and Taylor (2017). Standard works on lexicology include Lipka (1992), Halliday and Yallop (2007), Hanks (2007), Bauer (2021), and Jackson and Amvela (2022).

References

Altshuler, Daniel, Terence Parsons and Roger Schwarzschild. 2019. *A Course in Semantics*. Cambridge, MA: The MIT Press.
Bauer, Laurie. 2021. *Introduction to English Lexicology*. Edinburgh: Edinburgh University Press.
Cruse, David Alan. 1986. *Lexical Semantics*. Cambridge: Cambridge University Press.
Cruse, David Alan. 2004. *Meaning in Language: An Introduction to Semantics and Pragmatics*. Oxford: Oxford University Press.
Geeraerts, Dirl. 2015. Lexical Semantics. In James D. Wright (ed.), *International Encyclopedia of the Social & Behavioral Sciences*, 930–6. Oxford: Elsevier.
Goddard, Cliff and Anna Wierzbicka. 2013. *Words and Meanings: Lexical Semantics across Domains, Languages, and Cultures*. Oxford: Oxford University Press.
Halliday, Michael Alexander Kirkwood and Colin Yallop. 2007. *Lexicology: A Short Introduction*. London: Bloomsbury Publishing.
Hoffmann, Thomas. 1993. *Realms of Meaning: An Introduction to Semantics*. London: Longman.
Hanks, Patrick. 2007. *Lexicology: Critical Concepts in Linguistics*. London: Routledge.

Hurford, James and Brendan Heasley. 1983. *Semantics: A Coursebook*. Cambridge: Cambridge University Press.
Jackson, Howard and Etienne Z é Amvela. 2022. *An Introduction to English Lexicology: Words, Meaning and Vocabulary*. London: Bloomsbury Academic.
Kreidler, Charles. 2013. *Introducing English Semantics*. London: Routledge.
Leech, Geoffrey. 1974. *Semantics: The Study of Meaning*. London: Penguin Books.
Lipka, Leonhard. 1992. *An Outline of English Lexicology: Lexical Structure, Word Semantics, and Word-Formation*. Tübingen: Max Niemeyer Verlag.
Löbner, Sebastian. 2002. *Understanding Semantics*. London: Arnold.
Lyons, John. 1977. *Semantics* (2 Vols). Cambridge: Cambridge University Press.
Lyons, John. 1995. *Linguistic Semantics: An Introduction*. Cambridge: Cambridge University Press.
Palmer, Frank Robert. 1981. *Semantics*. Cambridge: Cambridge University Press.
Pustejovsky, James. 2006. Lexical Semantics: Overview. In Keith Brown (ed.), *The Encyclopedia of Language and Linguistics*, 5775. Amsterdam: Elsevier Ltd.
Riemer, Nick. 2010. *Introducing Semantics*. Cambridge: Cambridge University Press.
Taylor, John. 2017. Lexical Semantics. In Barbara Dancygier (ed.), *The Cambridge Handbook of Cognitive Linguistics*, 246–61. Cambridge: Cambridge University Press.

CHAPTER TWO

Lexical meaning

Preview

This chapter delves into the issue of lexical meaning in language, which is a fundamental concern of any theory of Lexical Semantics. This is because each theory approaches the description of lexical meaning in a unique way. The purpose is to demonstrate the significance of lexical meaning in language, as it pertains to the lexical items that make up the majority of items used in daily speech and writing. The chapter is structured as follows. The first section serves as the introduction, defining lexical meaning and identifying the elements that represent it in language. The second section discusses the levels of lexical meaning, distinguishing between literal and contextual meanings. The third section outlines various aspects of lexical meaning, including reference, sense, denotation and connotation. The fourth section categorizes types of lexical meaning as descriptive, expressive and social. The final section provides a summary of the analysis's findings and observations. The chapter concludes with recommendations for further reading.

Introduction

Lexical or central meaning refers to the meaning of a lexical item as it is defined in a dictionary. It is the aspect of meaning that is recorded in a lexicon or dictionary. Lexical meaning is often compared to grammatical meaning, which helps in understanding a lexical item through syntax. Typically, lexical meaning involves an open class of elements, whereas grammatical meaning is limited to a closed class of elements. Lexical meaning is linked to content or full lexical items like nouns, adjectives, verbs and adverbs, such as *table, blue, write, slowly*. The main purpose of content lexical items is to denote a thing, quality, state or action. On the other hand, grammatical meaning is related to functional or structural lexical items like articles, prepositions, conjunctions, tense and aspect, such as 'the', 'on' and 'but'. The main role of these lexical items is to show grammatical relationships. Lexical meaning is typically more detailed and intricate than grammatical meaning. Lexical meaning is associated with the lexicon, while grammatical meaning is related to syntax. The lexicon and grammar work together; every lexicon presupposes a grammar, and every grammar presupposes a lexicon. Content words can have both lexical and grammatical meanings. For instance, the lexical meaning of the noun *fly* refers to an object, whereas the grammatical meaning of the verb *fly* refers to a process.

Levels of lexical meaning

Two levels of lexical meaning can be distinguished. One is **literal** meaning, which is the meaning of a lexical item taken out of context. For example, the lexical item *sharp* means having a thin edge. The other is **contextual** meaning, which is the utterance meaning of a lexical item in actual speech. Context can be of two sorts: extra-linguistic or situational and linguistic. **Extra-linguistic context** refers to anything in the world outside of language that affects the interpretation of a lexical item. It is the immediate physical and social setting in which a lexical item occurs. For instance, in the sentence *I am freezing* the lexical item *freezing* means the weather is very cold, i.e., it is -5 degrees Celsius outside. **Linguistic context** refers to a set of lexical items that occur immediately before and/or after a lexical item in a phrase or sentence. For example, in *I broke a glass* the lexical item *glass* refers to an object, i.e., a container, whereas in *I drank a glass* the lexical item *glass* refers to liquid, i.e., content. It is evident that context is of vital importance, as it plays a role in the interpretation of a lexical item. When lexical items combine, the meaning of one item influences the meaning of the other, showing that the meaning of a lexical item is determined not only literally but also contextually.

The semantic import of a lexical item can vary from one context to another, and this variation is not random. It is endemic in the lexicon of any natural language. Lexical items have multiple meanings, and these meanings are manifested only in specific contexts. For example, the lexical item *sharp* displays multiple meanings. In *There was a sharp drop in prices*, it means sudden and rapid. In the sentence *This TV gives a very sharp picture*, it means clear and definite. In *She is a girl of sharp intelligence*, it means quick to notice, understand, or react to things. In *He was very sharp with me when I was late*, it means critical and severe. In *There was a sharp knock on the door*, it means loud and high in tone. In *The cheese has a distinctively sharp taste,* it means strong and slightly bitter. In *Tony is a very sharp dresser*, it means fashionable and new. In *His lawyer is a sharp operator*, it means clever but dishonest. In *He had a sharp pain in his chest*, it means strong and sudden. These examples demonstrate that meaning is flexible and open-ended. Any lexical item can convey new meanings or communicate new ideas depending on the context in which it is employed.

Practice 2.1

Use the provided lexical items in various contexts to showcase how they come to have certain meanings.

1. arm (n.)
2. date (n.)
3. drop (n.)
4. elegant (adj.)
5. turn (v.)

Aspects of lexical meaning

Lexical items are the primary bearers of meaning in language. Formulating a message is essentially a matter of selecting the appropriate lexical items. Each lexical item consists of both form and meaning. Generally, there are four aspects of meaning that we can recognize in lexical items: reference, sense, denotation and connotation. These aspects provide different ways of describing the meanings of lexical items. Reference is the entity that a lexical item points to in the world, sense is what a lexical item expresses, denotation is the strict dictionary meaning of a lexical item and connotation is the emotional association of a lexical item. These aspects create important contrasts within the meaning of a lexical item. Reference contrasts with sense, while denotation contrasts with connotation.

Reference

Reference is an aspect of meaning that a lexical item has through its ability to refer to an actual entity in the world. It is the specific real-world entity, called a **referent**, that a lexical item stands for on a specific occasion of use. For example, the reference of the lexical item *reader* points to an entity that is capable of reading. Reference concerns the ability of a lexical item to refer to real-world entities. A noun phrase in an utterance may or may not have a corresponding entity in the real world. For example, in the sentence *Yesterday we ate at the Italian restaurant*, the lexical item *restaurant* is referential, referring to a real-world entity. In the question *Can you recommend a good restaurant?* the lexical item *restaurant* is non-referential: the speaker does not have a specific real-world entity in mind to which the item refers. As the examples show, the same phrase can be referential in one utterance and non-referential in another. This demonstrates that reference is a property not of words or phrases as such but of linguistic expressions as they occur in actual discourse. The reference of a lexical item is the relationship between the item and the entity in the real world to which it refers.

Sense

Sense is an aspect of meaning that represents the signification or concept that a lexical item has. It is the meaning of a lexical item that is fundamental to its identity. It is the central meaning of a lexical item, the essential idea underlying it. This meaning is derived from the position it occupies within the language system or its semantic relationships with other items in the language. For example, the lexical item *reader* can be used in different senses. One sense is 'someone who reads something', another sense is 'a book designed for reading' and a further sense is 'a device that reads very small writing'. These examples show that differences in sense result in differences in denotation. This is why the term *sense* refers to the distinct meanings that a lexical item has. Each sense of the lexical item *reader* corresponds to a different denotation. The senses do not have any specific relationship between them. Unlike reference, which changes each time a lexical item is applied to a different referent, sense does not change when the lexical item takes on a different referent. For example, regardless of whether the referent of the lexical item *newsreader* is Jack or John, its sense remains the same: 'a person who reads the news on television or radio'.

TABLE 2.1 Reference versus sense

Reference	Sense
1. Reference is what a lexical item indicates.	1. Sense is what a lexical item expresses.
2. Reference deals with relationships between language and the world.	2. Sense deals with relationships inside the language.
3. Reference depends on the specific context in which a lexical item is used.	3. Sense does not depend on context.

Practice 2.2

In the following phrases, the lexical item *player* has the same referent (a person) but different senses. Write what each sense is.

1. a tennis player
2. a guitar player
3. a stage player
4. a market player
5. a card player

Denotation

Denotation is an aspect of meaning that signifies the literal, constant and fundamental meaning of a lexical item. It represents the objective relationship between a lexical item and the thing it refers to in the world. Denotation is akin to a dictionary definition that is universally agreed upon. It is the type of meaning that is most directly reflected in dictionary definitions of a lexical item, representing the relationship between a lexical item and the properties, actions or concepts it refers to. The denotation of a lexical item encompasses a broad class of things or the entire class of objects to which it accurately refers. In simpler terms, a lexical item's denotation is the class of potential objects, situations, etc. to which the item can refer. For instance, the lexical item *dog* denotes the class of all dogs, which are animals with four legs and a tail, often kept as a pet or trained for work. Denotation is therefore the linguistic meaning of a lexical item, distinct from connotation, which encompasses both social and affective meanings. The core meaning of a lexical item should be distinguished from its peripheral or variable aspects of meaning. While two or more lexical items may have the same denotation, they can have different significations. For example, the lexical item *father* is stylistically neutral, whereas *dad* is colloquial and *parenting* is bookish.

Connotation

Connotation is an aspect of meaning that signifies the figurative, cultural or emotional meaning evoked by a lexical item in specific contexts. It is the aspect of meaning that does not affect a lexical item's sense, reference or denotation. It refers to the semantic associations of a lexical item that do not alter the range of its potential referents. Unlike denotation which represents the literal meaning of a lexical item, connotation pertains to secondary factors such as its emotional impact, its level of formality or its character as a euphemism. For instance, the lexical item *dog* often carries positive connotations such as 'friend' or 'helper'. Connotation encompasses the additional meanings that a lexical item holds beyond its central meaning, heavily relying on subjective judgement. Take the example of the lexical item *police*. For some individuals, the connotation of *police* may be 'security', while for others, it may be 'harassment'.

TABLE 2.2 Denotation versus connotation

Denotation	Connotation
1. Denotation is the literal or primary meaning of a lexical item.	1. Connotation is the feelings or ideas which a lexical item suggests.
2. Denotation is the explicit meaning of a lexical item found in a dictionary.	2. Connotation is the implied or indirect meaning of a lexical item.
3. Denotation is objective, factual and verifiable meaning.	3. Connotation is subjective, emotional, personal, affective, attitudinal or expressive meaning.

In some cases, different lexical items have the same denotation but different connotations. For example, the denotations of *team*, *clique* and *group* are essentially the same as they all refer to a set of people. However, these items are not interchangeable because they have different connotations, each evoking a different emotion. A *team* is understood to be a set of people working towards the same aim, coming together to achieve a common goal, with a positive connotation. A *clique* is seen as a set of self-serving people who exclude outsiders, forming a narrow, exclusive circle held together by common interests, views or purposes, with a negative connotation. A *group* is viewed as a set of people related in some way to achieve organizational objectives, without a positive or negative association, having a neutral connotation.

The terms **reference** and **denotation** are not the same; they differ in two ways. First, a reference refers to a unique and real entity; the relation of a lexical item to a particular thing in the world. In contrast, denotation is the relationship between an entity and its property. For example, in *A wasp had flown in through the window* the noun phrases *a wasp* and *the window* refer to real-world things, with *wasp* and *window* denoting classes of concrete things. Referring terms refer to objects that bear names, with proper nouns denoting individuals, common nouns denoting sets of individuals, verbs denoting action, adjectives denoting individual properties and adverbs denoting action properties. The meaning of a sentence denotes a situation or event. Secondly, reference is a momentary relationship, while denotation is a stable relationship in language independent of lexical use.

For instance, the referent of the lexical item *musician* changes with context, such as Mozart or Beethoven, whereas its denotation remains the same as a person who writes or plays music professionally.

Practice 2.3

Study the following pairs carefully and show how the lexical items in each pair differ in connotation.

1. throw vs. hurl
2. thrifty vs. stingy
3. bargain vs. haggle
4. unique vs. peculiar
5. easygoing vs. lackadaisical

Types of lexical meaning

Meaning is what a lexical item signifies. The study of the meanings of lexical items, known as Lexical Semantics, explores not only what lexical items in the human language explicitly mean, but also what they implicitly convey. In other words, Lexical Semantics is concerned with both the proposition a lexical item conveys and the message it communicates. A thorough semantic analysis of a lexical item should consider all types of meaning. Semantic meanings can be categorized into three main types: descriptive, expressive and social. Descriptive meaning conveys factual information about a specific situation. It is the meaning found in dictionaries, also known as lexical or dictionary meaning. Expressive meaning reflects the subjective reactions of the speaker using the item, showing their emotions. Social meaning helps maintain social relationship during conversations, following the rules of social etiquette. Different lexical items are employed to represent these three types of meaning.

Descriptive meaning

The descriptive meaning of a lexical item is the fundamental meaning that it expresses. It includes both reference and truth, referring to something and stating its accuracy. It is the definition found in dictionaries. For example, the descriptive meaning of the lexical item *hawk* includes both referring to it as a bird and acknowledging its existence as a living creature. Descriptive meaning can also include characteristics of the item, such as the ability to hunt and kill other creatures for food. Descriptive meaning can be alternatively called propositional or ideational. A propositional meaning is the meaning of a lexical item that describes some state of affairs. As such, it has a truth value, which can be either true or false. An ideational meaning is the concept or idea that a lexical item expresses, helping listeners to identify its referent and determine its truth. Two lexical items may have similar basic meanings, but they can differ in their descriptive properties. For example, *big* and *colossal* refer to above-average size but differ in the dimension of intensity. *Colossal* implies extreme largeness or a large scale, whereas *huge* simply means very large.

Practice 2.4

The following pairs share the same referent but differ in descriptive details. Identify the difference.

1. kidnap   hijack
2. heal   cure
3. habit   custom
4. trip   journey
5. problem   trouble

Expressive meaning

The expressive meaning of a lexical item is its semantic quality, independent of the context in which it is used. It has a non-descriptive meaning that relates to speakers reflecting personal attitudes, feelings or sensations. Therefore, its use is simply a matter of personal judgement. The expressive meaning of a lexical item neither contributes to its propositional content nor influences its truth value. For example, the descriptive meaning of the lexical item *idiot* is a person, whereas its non-descriptive or expressive meaning is that of contempt. The most typical instances of lexical items with exclusively expressive meaning are interjections. For example, an utterance like *wow* expresses the speaker's amazement, *ouch* expresses mild pain and *ugh* is an expression of disgust. Some lexical items have both descriptive and expressive meanings, such as *Hi, honey, I'm home!* and *Happy birthday, sweetheart*! Two lexical items may describe the same situation, but they differ in expressiveness. Both *smart* and *intelligent* denote cleverness, but there is a difference in meaning. One becomes *smart* through effort, while *intelligence* is an innate quality of someone's makeup.

Expressive meaning corresponds to some extent with connotative, affective, emotive and attitudinal meanings. **Connotative** meaning refers to the additional meanings that a lexical item has that go beyond its denotative meaning. The denotative meaning of the lexical item *child* is what it literally means: a young human being. The connotative meaning of the lexical item *child* includes other general concepts associated with it, such as affection or nuisance. The **affective** meaning of a lexical item refers to the speaker's feelings towards a situation, which can differ from one person to another. For example, the affective meanings of the lexical items *dirty* and *filthy* convey different feelings. *Dirty* means unclean, whereas *filthy* means covered with filth. The use of each item signals the speaker's attitude or emotional state. The **emotive** meaning of a lexical item refers to the strong feelings, especially anger, that a subject, statement or use of language can evoke in people, such as *child abuse*. The **attitudinal** meaning of a lexical item reflects a person's interaction with the world, including manner, disposition, or feeling towards someone or something. Expressive meaning is contrasted with descriptive, denotative or referential meaning.

Practice 2.5

Below is a list of some common English interjections. Write what each interjection expresses.

1. ah!
2. alas!
3. hey!
4. ugh!
5. wow!

Social meaning

The social meaning refers to the association and implication that a lexical item or linguistic form carries based on social factors such as age, gender, class, ethnicity and more. These factors influence the meanings of lexical items and how they are interpreted in different social contexts. The fundamental insight is that language serves not only as a means of communication but also as a tool to express human social identity. For instance, the lexical items *masculine* and *feminine* carry significant social connotations, reflecting societal attitudes towards different genders. *Masculine* is linked to traits like strength, courage, independence, leadership and assertiveness, whereas *feminine* is associated with nurturing, empathy, sensitivity, grace and non-aggressive communication. This illustrates the crucial role that language plays in shaping and reflecting these perceptions. The language used to describe gender can impact how individuals are perceived and treated in various social settings. The lexical items used to describe genders can influence attitudes, behaviours and expectations towards individuals based on their gender. Exploring the social meanings of lexical items involves diving into complex topics such as gender identity, stereotypes and power dynamics within society.

Practice 2.6

Indicate how the social meanings of the following lexical items are associated with specific traits or defining features.

1. tomboy vs. sissy   gender
2. youthful vs. elderly   age
3. blue-collar vs. white-collar   class
4. macho vs. effeminate   gender
5. poverty vs. affluence   class

Another phenomenon in language is called **euphemism**. This phenomenon occurs when a lexical item or phrase is used instead of another to avoid being unpleasant, indecent or offensive. A lexical item or phrase that is considered unpleasant, indecent or offensive is described as being **politically incorrect**. On the other hand, the lexical item or phrase that avoids being unpleasant, indecent or offensive is described as being **politically correct**. For example, some people prefer to use the politically correct item *firefighter* instead of *fireman*, which can be seen as sexist. Linguistically speaking, the lexical item *firefighter* is a euphemism for *fireman*. Another example is using the politically correct phrase *senior citizen* instead of *old person*. Euphemisms are used in various aspects of language, including sexual activity (using *go to bed* instead of *intercourse*), bodily functions (using *the bathroom* instead of *defecating*), military (using *campaign* instead of *war*), death (using *pass away* instead of *dying*), politics (using *user fees* instead of *taxes*), religion (using *heck* instead of *hell*), and so on. The opposite of euphemism is **dysphemism**, which is a derogatory or unpleasant term used instead of a pleasant or neutral one.

Practice 2.7

The following lexical items are politically incorrect. Choose a euphemism for each to avoid using them.

1. sick
2. skinny
3. miserly
4. crippled
5. inquisitive

Summary

In this chapter, I have presented a broad outline of what lexical meaning is and what it covers. In the outline, I did three things. First, I identified the two levels that meaning falls into literal and contextual. Literal pertains to the strict or most basic meaning of a lexical item, whereas contextual pertains to the circumstances and surrounding items that can shed light on the meaning of a lexical item. Secondly, I addressed the four aspects that meaning has: reference, sense, denotation and connotation. Reference is the relation of a lexical item to something outside the language, i.e., in the world, whereas sense is a discrete representation of one aspect of the meaning of a lexical item. Denotation refers to the literal or primary meaning of a lexical item, whereas connotation refers to the ideas or feelings that the lexical item suggests. Thirdly, I distinguished the three types that meaning subsumes: descriptive, expressive and social. The descriptive meaning of a lexical item reveals the relationship between the item and its denotation. The expressive meaning of a lexical item discloses the attitudes held by speakers towards a given denotation. The social meaning of a lexical item reveals the social roles held by people in a community.

Key takeaways

- Lexical meaning refers to the specific meaning of a lexical item. It is the meaning that appears in a dictionary, where lexical items are defined and their meanings explained.

- Lexical meaning is influenced by both denotation and connotation. Denotation is the literal or dictionary meaning. Connotation is the associated or contextual meaning.

- Lexical meaning can vary across different contexts. Lexical items may have different meanings or shades of meaning depending on the context in which they are used.

- Lexical meaning is an important aspect of language production and comprehension. It allows for expressing ideas accurately and understanding intended meanings.

- Lexical meaning is flexible. The meaning of a lexical item is dynamic, namely it is constantly growing and changing to suit new experiences. It is **motivated** by the communicative purpose.

Further reading

Concerning lexical meaning, see Lyons (1995), Murphy (2010), Soames (2010), Asher (2011) and Kroeger (2018). Regarding the distinction between sense and reference, see McDowell (1977). Relating to the distinction between denotation and connotation, see Mill (2008). Referring to types of lexical meaning, see Palmer (1976), Leech (1981), Finegan (2008), Lyons (2002) and Loebner (2002).

References

Asher, Nicholas. 2011. *Lexical Meaning in Context: A Web of Words*. Cambridge: Cambridge University Press.
Finegan, Edward. 2008. *Language: Its Structure and Use*. Boston, MA: Thomson Wadsworth.
Kroeger, Paul. 2018. *Analyzing Meaning: An Introduction to Semantics and Pragmatics*. Berlin: Language Science Press.
Leech, Geoffrey. 1981. *Semantics: The Study of Meaning*. Harmondsworth: Penguin Books.
Loebner, Sebastian. 2002. *Understanding Semantics*. London: Routledge.
Lyons, John. 1995. *Linguistic Semantics: An Introduction*. Cambridge: Cambridge University Press.
Lyons, John. 2002. *Language and Linguistics: An Introduction*. Cambridge: Cambridge University Press.
McDowell, John. 1977. On the Sense and Reference of a Proper Name. *Mind* 86 (342): 159–85.
Mill, John Stuart. 2008. *Connotation and Denotation*. Helsinki: University of Helsinki. Retrieved 30 January 2009.
Murphy, Lynne. 2010. *Lexical Meaning*. Cambridge: Cambridge University Press.
Palmer, Frank. 1976. *Semantics: A New Outline*. Cambridge: Cambridge University Press.
Soames, Scott. 2010. *What Is Meaning?* Princeton, NJ, and Oxford: Princeton University Press.

CHAPTER THREE

Grammatical meaning

Preview

This chapter explores the concept of grammatical meaning in language, aiming to demonstrate its importance in aiding the reader's comprehension. Both lexical meaning and grammatical meaning play a role in conveying information, with examples including syntactic structures like the passive voice, morphological units such as gender and number, and phonological features like intonation. The chapter is structured as follows. The first section serves as an introduction, defining grammatical meaning and highlighting its significance in communication. The second section introduces semantic roles, outlining common roles and their defining characteristics. The third section discusses word order, illustrating how different word orders can conceptualize a situation in various ways and convey different meanings. The same words arranged in different orders signal different meanings. The final section summarizes the key points covered in the chapter. The chapter ends with some suggestions for further reading.

Introduction

Grammatical or structural meaning refers to the meaning of a lexical item within a grammatical context. It is the meaning of a lexical item based on its function within a sentence, rather than its reference to the world outside the sentence. In essence, it is the meaning that is inherent in a lexical item's syntactic behaviour. Grammatical meaning is linked to various word classes. For nouns, it is connected to number and gender. Number is a grammatical category used to analyse nouns that show contrasts like singular and plural. For example, both *child* and *children* have the same lexical meaning, but they differ grammatically in that one is singular, and the other is plural. With verbs, grammatical meaning is associated with tense, aspect and voice. Tense is a grammatical category used to analyse verbs that show contrasts such as present, past and future. For instance, *Kim sees Kate*, *Kim saw Kate* and *Kim will see Kate* all share the same lexical meaning, but they differ grammatically in that the first describes an event happening concurrently with the time of speaking, the second describes an event happening before the time of speaking, and the third describes an event happening after the time of speaking.

Grammatical meaning is conveyed in a phrase, clause or sentence by semantic roles and word order.

Semantic roles

One important aspect of grammatical meaning involves the semantic or thematic roles of lexical items in a sentence. This concept was first proposed by the Indian grammarian Panini. A **semantic role** is an underlying relationship that a participant has with the main verb in a clause, representing the specific relationships that exist between a verb and its arguments. The Lexical Semantics of a verb often consists of a list of semantic roles that apply to its arguments, showing how arguments are determined by the verb's meaning. The verb is the central component of any utterance, selecting the range of participant roles, which are then reduced to a set of labels specified as arguments. The purpose of semantic roles is to map the verb's arguments onto the syntactic roles of the subject and object, showing that lexical items are not just carriers of meaning but fulfil different roles within a situation. Semantic roles are crucial in how language is processed in the brain, providing a basis for clear statements about argument realization in language. Examining semantic roles is helpful because the same situation can be described differently in language. These roles are referred to by various names in linguistic literature, including participant roles, thematic relations and theta roles.

The following are the most widely used participant roles and the notions characterizing them.

- **Agent** is the volitional participant in an event who is seen as the animate initiator or doer of an action. In *Jane wrote a letter* and *A letter was written by Jane*, Jane is the participant who intentionally brings about the action denoted by the verb *write*.

- **Patient** or affected is the participant undergoing the effect of an action, often with a change of state. In *Kim baked a cake* and *A cake was baked by Kim*, *cake* is the participant that is acted upon by an agent or undergoes the change specified by the verb *bake*.

- **Theme** is the neutral role; the entity is neither acting itself nor being acted on by an agent. In *The pen rolled off the table*, *The pen is over there* and *The pen is in the drawer*, the *pen* is not an agent or a patient. It is moved as a result of an action denoted by the verb.

- **Causer** or force is an inanimate or non-volitional participant in an event that is the doer of the action. In *The wind blew the tent* and *The tent was blown by the wind*, the lexical item *the wind* is the participant that unintentionally causes the action of blowing.

- **Experiencer** is an animate participant who experiences an action or a state unintentionally. In *Lily has a headache, Lily saw the film, Lily felt sad* and *Lily heard a noise*, *Lily* is the entity that experiences the emotion, or the perception expressed by the verb.

- **Benefactive** or recipient is an animate participant who benefits from the action denoted by the verb. In *She cooked Leo a delicious meal*, *She sent Leo a postcard* and *She sang Leo a song*, Leo is the receiver of the action indicated by the verbs *cook, send* and *sing*.

- **Instrument** is something inanimate, concrete or abstract, used by an agent to carry out an action. In *The key opened the door* and *He opened the door with a key*, the *key* is the instrument used by the agent to bring about the action designated by the verb *open*.

- **Goal** is the entity towards which something moves, in either a physical or an abstract sense. In *Jack travelled to London* and *Jack reached London after midnight*, London is the entity or the location in the direction in which Jack moves.

- **Source** is the entity from which something moves, in either a physical or an abstract sense, as in *Jack flew in from London* and *The dictionary gives a lot of information*, London and dictionary are the entities described as the starting points or origins of the events.

- **Location** is the place in which an action takes place or where something is situated. In *The crowd gathered at the central station*, and *The cat is lying on the floor*, *at the central station*, and *on the floor* are the places where the situation takes place.

- **Time** is the temporal dimension in which the action or the situation denoted by the verb is carried out. In *Tomorrow is her birthday* and *The bell rings at noon*, the adverb of time *tomorrow* and *noon* represent the temporal placement of the events.

- **Possessor** is the entity that owns something or has a particular quality at one's disposal. In *Alice owns two mobile phones* and *Alice has two mobile phones*, Alice is the possessor of the object of possession, which is a mobile phone in the examples.

From the above discussion, we can see that semantic roles are descriptions of syntactic elements and their functions in a sentence. They indicate the parts played by participants in a situation or event. The same situation might be described in different ways; so looking at semantic roles is useful in thinking about alternative ways to describe the same situation. The two most common roles are agent and patient. The agent is usually, but not always, the subject, while the patient is the thing that is acted upon and usually the direct object. For example, in the sentence *John hit Jill*. John is the agent and the subject of the action, while Jill is the patient and the direct object of the action. In *Jill hit John*, the situation is reversed, with Jill as the agent and subject, and John as the patient and direct object. In *Jane watered the flowers*, Jane is the agent and subject, whereas in *Jane smelled the flowers*, Jane is still the subject but the experiencer of the action. In short, the type of verb not only determines the syntactic functions of the participants in a sentence but also helps determine their semantic roles.

Practice 3.1

In the sentences that follow, identify the semantic role of each element that is underlined.

1. The <u>winter</u> of 2010 was mild.
2. The <u>guards</u> stopped the crowd.
3. <u>He</u> was sent a postcard by them.
4. This <u>path</u> is swarming with ants.
5. They painted the walls with a <u>brush</u>.
6. My <u>father</u> always feels proud of me.
7. The <u>mansion</u> was destroyed in the war.
8. They made the new fences from <u>stones</u>.
9. The <u>hurricane</u> demolished possessions.
10. They sat on the <u>couch</u> watching football.

Word order

Another important aspect of grammatical meaning has to do with word order. **Word order**, also known as linear order, refers to the arrangement of syntactic constituents within phrases, clauses or sentences. It dictates the sequence in which the lexical items appear in a sentence. The order of lexical items in an English sentence is highly significant. Ignoring word order means losing access to a whole dimension of meaning. Changing word order often results in a change in meaning, sometimes used to achieve a special effect. Therefore, differences in word order lead to differences in meaning. Speakers do not present information to listeners in a random or unstructured manner. They package information in a way that allows listeners to interpret what is encoded in the syntax. This implies that the syntax of a sentence encodes its semantic meaning. A sentence describes a situation in the world, making a specific contribution.

To understand the meaning of a lexical item, one has to look at its behaviour in a sentence.

Positions of lexical items

One important aspect of the behaviour of a lexical item is its position in a sentence. It is crucial to consider where the lexical item is located within a phrase, clause or sentence. Therefore, the position that a lexical item occupies plays a significant role in its interpretation in a specific communicative situation. English places a strong emphasis on the placement of lexical items to effectively communicate meaning. Often, a change in position can result in a change in meaning. The speaker can envision a situation in various ways and select the appropriate word order to convey it in discourse. The choice between two phrases, clauses or sentences, for example, is based not solely on their conceptual content but also on the specific arrangement of their words. The speaker can describe a given scene in multiple ways, and rely on a variety of symbolic resources to encode them. Each word order represents a distinct semantic structure, and therefore the available alternatives are not considered synonymous. Each word order has a meaning of its own unique meaning and serves a specific purpose in language.

Consider the examples below indicating how a shift in position signals a difference in meaning.

(1) a. He had his car polished.
   b. He had polished his car.

The sentences contain the same wording, but each represents a specific perspective that the speaker imposes on the scene, resulting in a different meaning. The difference between them is not based on formal rules; it is solely a matter of conceptualization: the ability to portray them in different ways. The first sentence implies that someone else did the polishing, meaning I arranged for somebody to polish my car. The second sentence means that he polished it, indicating he polished his car. Clearly, a change in the position of the word *polish* in the sentences changes the meaning significantly. A difference in position leads to a difference in meaning.

(2) a. I say what I mean.
   b. I mean what I say.

Although the sentences contain the same lexical items, their meanings differ. Both convey the idea of honesty and sincerity in communication, but they emphasize different aspects. The first is used to convey I speak my mind; I don't use roundabout euphemisms, but instead, speak directly and honestly without hidden meanings or ulterior motives. It sometimes implies that the speaker will be blunt and even rude. It suggests that the speaker's words accurately reflect their thoughts and intentions. On the other hand, the second is used to convey I don't idly threaten, I will follow through on what I say I will do. It implies that the speaker's words are not frivolous or insincere, and they are meant to be taken seriously. Essentially, the first pertains to the clarity and directness of communication, while the second pertains to the integrity and seriousness of the communicated message. Both phrases highlight the importance of honesty and sincerity in communication.

(3) a. They genuinely need to be solid.
b. They need to be solid genuinely.

The sentences contain the same lexical items, but they convey different meanings. The difference lies in the emphasis and focus of the sentence. In the first sentence, the emphasis is on the need for something to be solid, with the word *genuinely* adding emphasis to the statement, meaning they need to be firm. In the second sentence, the emphasis is on the genuine nature of the need itself. The placement of *genuinely* shifts the focus to the sincerity or authenticity of the need, meaning they must be firm honestly or sincerely. In this case, the word order is important not to convey feeling or tone, but to impart a specific sense or interpretation. Clearly, using the same lexical items in a different order causes a significant change in meaning.

Practice 3.2

In the following sentences, changing the position of *only* can cause drastic changes in meaning.

1. Only I asked him a question about history.
2. I only asked him a question about history.
3. I asked only him a question about history.
4. I asked him only a question about history.
5. I asked him a question only about history.

Another aspect of the behaviour of a lexical item relates to its flexibility in the phrase of which it is a part. This is manifested by reversible and non-reversible lexical pairs.

Reversible lexical pairs

Certain pairs of English lexical items, when used together, demonstrate reversibility: the ability to change or switch. This involves rearranging the usual order of the lexical items in either direction. A reversible lexical pair is a pair of items that can be interchanged, causing differences in meaning. This phenomenon is common and understandable. Conceptually, a speaker can view a situation from various perspectives. Linguistically, a speaker can select the appropriate items, arranging them in a meaningful way to represent the situation. The difference in meaning depends on which item serves as the main focus in the phrase. This aligns with the idea that a change in form always indicates a change in meaning. Shifting the position of items in a phrase alters the meaning or indicates a difference in how the phrase functions in discourse. Using these lexical pairs is helpful for enhancing the meaning of spoken and written sentences. They provide specificity to the message and contribute to a more fluent delivery of language.

Consider the examples below indicating how a swap of lexical items in a phrase signals a difference in meaning.

(4) a. sugar cane
 b. cane sugar

The phrases have the same wording, but each receives a specific interpretation and serves a different function in language. Each phrase has a specific purpose in the language. In the first phrase, *sugar cane* refers to 'a tall tropical plant with thick stems from which sugar is extracted', making it the plant from which sugar is produced. In the second phrase, *cane sugar* refers to 'sugar obtained from the juice of sugar cane', making it the end product derived from a specific cane plant. It is clear that reversing the order can make a difference in meaning or reference.

Here is a brief list of some of the most useful reversible lexical pairs in English. These pairs can be reversed, resulting in a difference in both meaning and usage. *Water tap*: tap from which water comes/*tap water*: water that comes from a tap, *book exam*: exam that is based on a book/*exam book*: book to read for an exam, *meat stew*: stew containing meat/*stew meat*: meat used in a stew, *bag tea*: tea made from a tea bag/*tea bag*: bag containing a portion of tea, *cage bird*: bird kept in a cage/*bird cage*: cage for holding a bird, *wine box*: box containing wine/*box wine*: wine sealed inside a box.

Practice 3.3

The following compounds differ in combinatorial arrangement and semantic value. Explain what each means.

1. a. guest house   b. house guest
2. a. wall paper   b. paper wall

3. a. leather shoe   b. shoe leather
4. a. flower garden   b. garden flower
5. a. houseboat   b. boathouse

Non-reversible lexical pairs

Certain English lexical items, when paired together, exhibit non-reversibility: cannot be altered, meaning impossible to change their order. This involves placing the lexical items in a pair in a fixed order. A non-reversible lexical pair is a pair of items used together in a stable order that is logically consistent. In many ways, these lexical pairs are similar to collocations and idiomatic expressions. They are usually joined by the conjunctions *and* or *or*, and belong to the same part of speech, such as nouns like *knife and fork*, adjectives like *sick and tired*, or verbs like *give and take*. Their interpretation is different; some pairs are literal like *rich and famous*, while others are figurative like *nip and tuck*, which means very closely contested, i.e. neck and neck. The order of the elements in the lexical pairs cannot be reversed. These lexical pairs are learned through custom and usage. When the order of the elements in a pair is reversed, the pair sounds odd. There are some rules governing the order. (i) There is a logic to a lot of these collocations as in *crime and punishment*. (ii) The semantically bigger thing comes first as in *fish and chips*. (iii) The semantically better thing comes first as in *pros and cons*. (iv) The longer a lexical item goes last as in *salt and pepper*. (v) Adjective order as in *tall and thin*.

Consider the examples below indicating how a swap of lexical items in a phrase sounds awkward.

(5) a. signed and sealed
     b. *sealed and signed

The phrases have the same wording but differ in order. Only the first one makes sense. A document is signed first and then sealed in an envelope. *Signed and sealed* means finished and official, or officially approved or verified. All the necessary documents have been signed. The second phrase sounds awkward because one cannot sign a document when it is already sealed inside an envelope. The same applies to *cause and effect*. The order *effect and cause* is not natural because one cannot have an effect until there is a cause for the effect.

Here is a brief list of some of the most useful non-reversible lexical pairs in English. These pairs are irreversible, meaning their order cannot be changed. *Rise and fall, flesh and blood, right or wrong, suit and tie, food and drink, front and centre, supply and demand, lost and found, trial and error, give and take, in and out, read and write, wait and see, up and down, hammer and nail, body and soul, bread and butter, bride and groom, by and large, husband and wife, law and order, life or death, lock and key, man and wife, profit and loss, pros and cons, to and fro, war and peace, sooner or later, sweet and sour, black and white, high and low, thick and thin, neat and clean, wet and dry*, etc.

Practice 3.4

Here are a few instances of lexical pairs that are invariably compatible. The other half is absent in each. Finish it.

1. cup and   -----
2. back and   -----
3. dead or   -----
4. safe and   -----
5. needle and -----

Summary

In this chapter, I have provided a brief account of what grammatical meaning is and what it encompasses. Grammatical meaning refers to the aspect of meaning that indicates grammatical relationships or functions of lexical items. In this account, I have done three things. First, I have clarified what grammatical meaning entails and how it is expressed in language. Secondly, I have addressed the concept of semantics roles, which are the various roles that a noun phrase may assume in relation to the action or state described by the main verb of a sentence. I have discussed the major semantic roles or thematic relations in which grammatical meaning is manifested. Thirdly, I have discussed word order, which refers to the arrangement of lexical items in a phrase, clause or sentence are placed. Word order is crucial in both speaking and writing, as it determines the coherence of the message. Changes in word order can alter the meaning conveyed. By rearranging the lexical items in different ways, a writer or speaker can convey different meanings or achieve different communicative goals.

Key takeaways

- Grammatical meaning is the meaning of a lexical item as it appears in a grammatical context. It refers to the meaning conveyed by the grammatical patterns used in a language.

- Grammatical meaning is influenced by the roles and orders of lexical items in a sentence. Semantic roles are not inherent properties of lexical items but are relational notions.

- Grammatical meaning is essential for effective communication. It is important for language users to express themselves effectively and comprehend spoken or written language.
- Grammatical meaning can vary depending on context, requiring careful analysis by language users. The same lexical item can have a different role depending on its position in a sentence.
- Grammatical meaning is affected by alternation. This is manifested by the alteration of the normal order of the lexical items, accompanied by ensuing meaning differences.

Further reading

On the subject of grammatical meaning, see Mohanan and Wee (1999) and Bulter (2010). In connection with semantic/thematic roles, see Dowty (1991), Frawley (1992), Berk (1999), Fillmore (2015) and Perini (2019). With regard to word order, see Lehmann (1975), Tomlin (1986) and Herring (1990).

References

Berk, Lynn. 1999. *English Syntax: From Word to Discourse*. Oxford: Oxford University Press.
Bulter, Alastair. 2010. *The Semantics of Grammatical Dependencies*. Leeds: Emerald Group Publishing.
Dowty, David R. 1991. Thematic Proto-Roles and Argument Selection. *Language* 67 (3): 547–619.
Fillmore, Charles. 2015. *Form and Meaning in Language*. Volume I, Papers on Semantic Roles.
Frawley, William. 1992. *Linguistic Semantics*. New York: Routledge.
Herring, Susan Catherine. 1990. Information Structure as a Consequence of Word Order Type. Proceedings of the Sixteenth Annual Berkeley Linguistics Society, 163–74.
Lehmann, Winfred. 1975. A Discussion of Compound and Word Order. In Charles, Ning Li (ed.), *Word Order and Word Order Change*, 149–62. Austin, TX: University of Texas Press.
Mohanan, Tara and Lionel Wee (eds.). 1999. *Grammatical Semantics: Evidence for Structure in Meaning*. Stanford, CA: CSLI Publications, affiliated with the Center for the Study of Language and Information at Stanford University.
Perini, Mario. 2019. *Thematic Relations: A Study in the Grammar-Cognition Interface*. New York: Springer.
Tomlin, Russell. 1986. *Basic Word Order: Functional Principles*. London: Croom Helm.

PART TWO

Prior approaches to lexical meaning

In this part, I will examine the role that lexical meaning played in earlier approaches. The goal is to uncover the methods they used to define meaning. This part is divided into three chapters. Chapter 4 focuses on Traditional Lexical Semantics, where the meaning of a lexical item is understood in two ways: either by linking it to an object in the real world, a theory called reference, or by knowing the conditions under which it would be true, a theory called truth conditions. Chapter 5 discusses Structural Lexical Semantics, where the meaning of a lexical item is demonstrated through either the groupings of lexical items, a theory called lexical fields, or the relationships it has with the other items in the language, a theory called sense relations. Chapter 6 delves into Generative Lexical Semantics, which examines the meaning of a lexical item in three ways: by analysing its components, a theory called Componential Analysis, reducing it to a set of semantic primitives, a theory called Natural Semantic Metalanguage, and breaking it down into ontological categories such as events, states, places, amounts, things and property, a theory called Conceptual Semantics.

Outline

4 Traditional Lexical Semantics 39
   Introduction 39
   Strategies 41
      Reference 41
      Truth conditions 44
   Critical appraisal 46
   Summary 47
   Key takeaways 48
   Further reading 48
   References 49

5 Structural Lexical Semantics 51
   Introduction 51
   Strategies 52
      Lexical fields 53
      Sense relations 55
      Paradigmatic relations 56
         Antonymy 57
         Polysemy 59
         Synonymy 60
         Taxonomy 62
      Syntagmatic relations 63
         Anomaly 64
         Collocation 65
         Colligation 66
         Idiomaticity 67
   Critical appraisal 68
   Summary 70
   Key takeaways 70
   Further reading 70
   References 71

6 Generative Lexical Semantics 73
  Introduction 73
  Strategies 75
    Componential Analysis 75
    Natural Semantic Metalanguage 77
    Conceptual Semantics 79
  Critical appraisal 80
  Summary 82
  Key takeaways 83
  Further reading 83
  References 83

CHAPTER FOUR

Traditional Lexical Semantics

Preview

This chapter explores the traditional approaches to the study of lexical meaning, aiming to provide a general understanding of how traditionalists perceive lexical meaning. The task of the chapter is to introduce readers to fundamental concepts in the study of lexical meaning. To that end, the chapter is structured as follows. The first section serves as the introduction, reviewing Traditional Lexical Semantics and its common assumptions that impact the analysis of language and meaning. These assumptions are rooted in Traditional Semantics. The second section introduces two theories: reference and truth conditions, emphasizing the shared axioms that guide their approach to lexical meaning. The third section offers a critical appraisal of the traditional theories, examining their practicality and highlighting their limitations. The final section recaps the main ideas presented in the chapter.

Introduction

Traditional Lexical Semantics is associated with the work of such philosophers as Socrates, Plato and Aristotle. It is part of traditional grammar and based on **prescriptivism**, which emphasizes enforcing rules on language usage. Prescriptivism involves laying down norms for language usage. It is characterized by a concern for proper or correct usage. It regards grammar as a structured and conventional method of human communication, ignoring actual usage in favour of prescriptive rules. Lexical items are considered names or labels for things and parts of speech are defined based on meaning. For instance, the meaning of the lexical item *Susan* is simply the person it refers to in the real world. Traditional theories of meaning prioritize objective over subjective experience. Objective experiences are mind-independent, reflecting real-world events, whereas subjective experiences are mind-dependent, representing the cognitive impact of human experiences.

Assumptions

- Each lexical item in the language is associated with just one unique and discrete meaning. Language users generally rely on dictionaries to identify this meaning. However, this assumption is mistaken, as a lexical item can have multiple meanings that are revealed in different contexts. Meanings can change faster than they can be recorded in dictionaries, making lexical meanings flexible, imprecise and fluid. For example, the verb *fire* can express multiple meanings: (i) 'to burn or ignite', as in *He fired the wood*; (ii) 'to shoot bullets from a gun', as in *He fired three shots*; (iii) 'to discharge from one's employment', as in *He has just been fired from his job*; (iv) 'to make someone very excited', as in *The story fired our imagination*; (v) 'to ask someone a lot of questions very quickly', as in *The reporters fired non-stop questions at him*.

- The meanings of individual lexical items are often treated separately or in isolation, following an atomistic approach to lexical meaning. However, this assumption is mistaken as lexical items typically enter into various sense relationships with other lexical items in the language. In language, the meanings of lexical items are interdependent. For example, it is impossible to know the meaning of *glimpse* without also knowing the meaning of the lexical item *glance*. Both lexical items relate to vision, but they differ in the distinction between a chance happening and a wilful act. The verb *glimpse* means 'to see someone or something for a moment without getting a complete view of them', as in *I glimpsed a figure at the window*. *Glimpse* happens by chance. The verb *glance* means 'to look at someone or something for a short time', as in *He glanced at his watch*. *Glance* is a wilful act.

- Literal meaning is often considered the norm, distinct from the non-literal one. Only literal meaning can be true or false, and is included in the semantic structure of a lexical item. Non-literal language is seen as anomalous, and is typically excluded from the semantic structure of a lexical item. However, this assumption is mistaken because lexical items can have both literal and non-literal meanings. For example, a current of air blowing through a window can be described as either a *draft* or a *breeze*, but with a difference in non-literal meaning. A *draft* is cold and undesired, making one feel uncomfortable, as in *I feel a draft coming in from under the door*, while a *breeze* is a light, gentle wind that is cool and desired, as in *The breeze rustled the papers on her desk*.

Strategies

A prevailing tendency in Traditional Lexical Semantics is the **denotational** approach. According to this approach, the meaning of a lexical item in a given language is determined in terms of the relation between the item and the thing it refers to. Specifically, it is the relation between language and the world. Two aspects of denotation are distinguished: extension and intension. The extension of a lexical item is the set of referents it properly applies to, or the range of referents covered by a particular lexical item. For example, the extension of the lexical item *dog* includes all types of dogs like *guide dogs, lapdogs, sheepdogs, sniffer dogs, tracker dogs* etc. The intension of a lexical item is the property or properties that allow its extension to be determined. For instance, the intension of the lexical item *dog* includes properties like assisting, accompanying, guarding etc. Denotation is the basic meaning of a lexical item, contrasting with connotation, which refers to the ideas or emotions suggested by a lexical item. Denotatively, *home* is defined as a dwelling house, while connotatively it has associations of domesticity and warmth.

The major denotational theories in Traditional Lexical Semantics are reference and truth conditions.

Reference

One way of defining lexical meaning in Traditional Lexical Semantics pertains to reference. Meaning is equated with reference, where the meaning of a lexical item resides in the relationship between the item and aspects of the outside world. In Traditional Lexical Semantics, language is seen as corresponding to the external world in an almost literal sense. Meaning does not reside in the mind of the speaker, but rather is placed in an extra-linguistic reality. The meaning of a lexical item involves applying it appropriately to an object in the world. A reference designates a specific person, place or thing that a speaker identifies when using a lexical item. Accordingly, the meaning of *bus* refers to buses and nothing else, with the referent of the lexical item *bus* being the vehicle itself, a real, physical object in the real world. This way, reference is opposed to sense, as it concerns relations external to language, specifically the relationship between a lexical item and an entity in the external world, while sense concerns relations internal to language, focusing on the relationship of a lexical item to other lexical items in the same language or linguistic system.

Axioms

- Meaning is a purely language-external phenomenon. In this sense, meaning equates with denotation, referring to objects in the external world. Meaning resides in the relationship between a lexical item and the explicit entity that it designates. Similarly, meaning equates with the literal meaning of a lexical item, the kind of meaning found in dictionary definitions. Other aspects of meaning, such as connotations and usage, are excluded. In virtue of the reference theory, the two lexical items *referee* and *umpire* refer to a person who ensures that the rules are followed in a sports game. However, there is a difference in usage that the theory disregards. The lexical item *referee* controls contact sports games such as football, basketball and handball. The lexical item *umpire*, by contrast, controls non-contact sports games such as cricket, tennis and baseball.

- Lexical items having the same denotation are synonymous. Synonymy denotes a semantic relationship of sameness in meaning between lexical items. In light of the reference theory, the two lexical items *soldier* and *warrior* denote men of war. As such, they are considered synonymous because they share the same denotation. However, there is a difference in meaning that the reference theory ignores. The lexical item *soldier* is a person who serves in the army. To be a soldier is to fight for a living, it is an occupation. The lexical item *warrior* is a person who fights when the occasion arises. A warrior is not a fighter by profession. He does not work for money. As is clear, each lexical item has a meaning of its own. These nuances of meaning are important to set lexical items apart. The difference is borne out by the communicative context in which the lexical items are used.

An example

In terms of the theory of reference, the meaning of a lexical item is what it points out in the world. The object denoted by a lexical item is called its referent, correlating lexical items with actual objects in the world. This is best illustrated with an example of a proper name. Consider the proper name Shakespeare. The purpose of a name is to refer to an individual. In this case, Shakespeare is the man whom the name represents. It is the object for which the name stands. The name has a truth value because there is an object in the world with that name. The referent of the lexical item Shakespeare is a real, physical entity referred to by linguistic means. This function, **referential** meaning, contrasts with **sense**, which concerns the essential idea underlying a lexical item. Although the referential function of language is fundamental to communication and a good starting point in the investigation of meaning, it has limitations as we will see in the upcoming section.

Practice 4.1

The underlined lexical items have similar denotations. Each item, though, carries a distinct connotation. Point it out.

1. They cannot <u>interfere</u> in family affairs.
   They cannot <u>intervene</u> in family affairs.

2. The new employee strikes us as a <u>clever</u> man.
   The new employee strikes us as an <u>intelligent</u> man.

3. After her mother's death, she felt <u>alone</u>.
   After her mother's death, she felt <u>lonely</u>.

4. The woman sitting by the window is <u>beautiful</u>.
   The woman sitting by the window is <u>pretty</u>.

5. He was <u>upset</u> because he dropped the laptop.
   He was <u>angry</u> because he dropped the laptop.

Depending on the context in which they are used, lexical items can be used referentially or non-referentially. A referring lexical item, such as a noun phrase, is used to identify or point to a specific individual or object in the world. In this way, the hearer of the lexical item can understand the speaker's intention. In English, referring lexical items often contain a definite article like *the key*, demonstratives like *this key*, personal pronouns like *my key* and adverbials like in *the key here*. In all these examples, the speaker is referring to a specific object. On the other hand, a non-referring lexical item, such as a noun phrase, refers to a type or category. It provides general information about the thing rather than a particular instance. In English, non-referring lexical items often contain indefinite articles like *a key*, quantifiers like *any key*, negation markers like *no key* and bare plurals like *keys*. While these items do of course contribute meaning to the sentences in which they appear, they do not refer to specific individual entities in the world. Reference then is the act performed by speakers to direct the listeners' attention to specific entities in the external world.

Practice 4.2

Indicate whether the underlined lexical items in the sentences below are referring or non-referring.

1. A beagle is a <u>dog</u>.
2. The <u>tiger</u> hunts by night.
3. No <u>cat</u> likes being bathed.
4. All <u>musicians</u> are emotional.
5. This <u>city</u> has pollution problems.

That <u>dog</u> is a beagle.
<u>Tigers</u> hunt by night.
The <u>cat</u> likes being bathed.
Those <u>musicians</u> are emotional.
Every <u>city</u> has pollution problems.

Truth conditions

The other way of defining lexical meaning in Traditional Lexical Semantics pertains to truth conditions. It is a type of semantics associated with Donald Davidson. Truth-conditional semantics is based on the notion that the core meaning of any lexical item is its truth conditions. Meaning is defined in terms of the conditions in the real world under which a lexical item is used to make a true statement. It focuses on the circumstances in the external world under which the meaning of a lexical item is true. It sees the meaning of a lexical item as being the same as or reducible to its truth conditions. This is a view that focuses on the relationship between language and the world instead of the relationship between language and the mind. For example, the meaning of *Snow is white* is true if and only if snow is white. Knowing this condition is necessary for understanding the meaning of the statement. Thus, to give an account of the meaning of a statement is to specify the conditions under which the situation described would be true or false. The condition is the requirement that the world must satisfy in order for the statement to be true. This is in contrast to approaches that define meaning in terms of the use of lexical items in communication, or the speaker's role in describing a scene.

Axioms

- Meaning resides in the conditions of objective external reality against which a lexical item can be judged true or false. In this sense, meaning equates with denotation, considering language as corresponding to the world in a literal sense. In this respect, the truth-conditional theory of meaning is in opposition to the use-conditional theory of meaning, whereby the meaning is a matter of the way a lexical item is put to use by competent users. In terms of the truth-conditional theory, the two lexical items *wound* and *injury* refer to physical damage to the body, and are freely interchangeable. However, there is a difference in connotation which the theory ignores. The lexical item *wound* is the result of an intentional action caused by a weapon, as in *The victim suffered a severe stab wound*. The lexical item *injury*, on the other hand, is the result of an accident caused by a crash, as in *The train passenger sustained a serious injury in the crash*.

- Lexical items sharing the same truth conditions are synonymous. A synonym is a lexical item that means exactly or nearly the same as another lexical item in a given language. This occurs when two lexical items share the set of conditions under which they are said to be true and can be substituted freely. For example, the lexical items *brawl* and *fight* are truth-conditionally the same but use-conditionally different. So, they cannot be used interchangeably. Although both lexical items refer to physical conflicts, they differ in the degree of violence involved. A *brawl* is a noisy quarrel involving a group of people, usually in a public place, and may involve pushing, shoving and insulting, typically less serious than a fight. A *fight*, by contrast, is an altercation between two or more individuals, while may involve punching, kicking and using weapons, and is more serious than a brawl.

An example

Let us examine the lexical item *bird*. For an entity to belong to this category, it must meet the following truth conditions: [feathers], [wings], [legs], [ability to lay eggs], [ability to build a nest], [ability to fly], [ability to sing] and so on. Based on these conditions, a sparrow, falcon and robin fall into the category as they possess most of these characteristics. Each condition is necessary in that every member of the category bird must possess them. Additionally, all conditions together are sufficient, meaning every member of the bird category must have all of these traits. In contrast, a penguin, ostrich and chicken would be outside the category for lacking some of the truth conditions such as the ability to fly. This demonstrates that understanding the meaning of a lexical item involves knowing the specific conditions it must meet to be considered true. We have a mental definition of what a bird is. It is important to observe a real-world object to determine if it meets these conditions. If an object meets all these conditions, it is considered true. If it does not, then it is false. While this theory provides clarity on meaning, it also has some limitations, which we will explore in the next section.

Practice 4.3

The following pairs of nouns are truth-conditionally similar but use-conditionally different. How?

1. ache vs. pain
2. hotel vs. hostel
3. salary vs. wage
4. award vs. reward
5. holiday vs. vacation

Critical appraisal

Traditional Lexical Semantics is a branch of traditional linguistics, with a main focus on structure. In Traditional Lexical Semantics, language is treated as an isolated system, separate from human cognitive abilities and human interaction with the physical and social world. This view is consistent with the modularity thesis, where language is made up of subsystems (lexicon, morphology, phonology, syntax) with specific tasks considered separate linguistic components that function independently of one another. Traditional Lexical Semantics adopts two theories. Under the reference theory, the meaning of a lexical item is referential, the object to which a lexical item refers. Under the truth-conditional theory, the meaning of a lexical item consists of the conditions under which it is true. The semantic value of a lexical item can be reduced to an objective characterization of the situation described. Both theories of meaning are denotational, relating to dictionary meanings.

The adoption of the two theories to describe lexical meaning has the following limitations.

- Propositional meaning is the centre of attention. The **propositional** meaning of a lexical item is that part of its meaning which determines its truth conditions. In this way, the reference theory excludes non-propositional meaning including descriptive, expressive and social content. In light of the two theories, the adjectives *false* and *untrue* share the same proposition: lack of veracity. In usage, however, they are different which they ignore. The former as in *She was charged with giving false evidence in court* is more disapproving than the latter as in *The story was completely untrue*. The non-propositional content of *false* includes the notion of deliberateness.

- Concrete entities with truth conditions are the main focus of analysis. Abstract entities without referents in the physical world are excluded. In virtue of the two theories, the two nouns *shade* and *shadow* share the same referent, a dark area that light does not reach, making them equal in meaning. In usage, however, they are different. *Shade* refers to any dark area in which sunlight or other bright light is blocked, as in *It's so hot out, let's sit in the shade of the pine tree*. *Shadow* refers to the dark shape that appears on a surface when an object blocks sunlight or other light, as in *The ship's sail cast its shadow on the water*.

- When two lexical items occur in the same position, they are in free alternation, which is the substitutability of one lexical item for another in a given environment. Given the reference and truth-conditional theories, the two verbs *steal* and *rob* mean theft, and are considered free alternatives. In usage, however, they are distinguishable. *Steal* is used in the case of thefts that are considered small in volume and focuses on something specific, as in *The thief stole a necklace*. *Rob* is used in the case of thefts that are considered high in volume and focuses on the place or person from which the thing is taken, as in *The gang robbed the bank*.

- Both theories only consider the relation between a lexical item and the world, ignoring the impact of context on interpretation. They fail to acknowledge the significance of the context in which a lexical item is used, thus missing the essence of communication. For instance, the lexical item *plain* has multiple meanings, but to determine its intended meaning, we need to consider the surrounding items. In *plain dress*, it means 'simple and undecorated', whereas in *plain fact* it means 'honest and direct'. These examples illustrate how lexical items can have nuanced meanings that are clarified by context.

Due to these limitations, the reference and truth-conditional theories are inadequate in addressing all semantic challenges. This gap has led to the development of a new theory of meaning, called Cognitive Lexical Semantics. In this cognitive framework, explored in Part III, the central concept is the relationship between meaning and the mind. Meaning is viewed as a mental construct, with a focus on the connection between language and mental representations of the external world. Meaning is considered to be inherent to the mind, resulting from human cognitive abilities. It is seen as a mapping from conceptual structures to lexical items, derived from the context of language use by activating elements of conceptual structures. Meaning is synonymous with conceptualization and is grounded in perception. Cognitive Lexical Semantics delves into the role of human perception and conceptualization, aiming to explain lexical phenomena through general cognitive strategies like prototype, frame, construal, metaphor, metonymy and more.

Summary

In this chapter, I have provided a brief overview of the Traditional Lexical Semantics, focusing on two theories: reference and truth conditions. Under the reference theory, a lexical item's meaning is tied to connection with a real-world object. Under the truth-conditional theory, a lexical item's meaning is equivalent to its truth conditions. Both theories emphasize denotation, where meaning arises from the relationship between a lexical item and a non-linguistic entity. Both theories regard meaning as objective, with truth contingent on correspondence to an objective reality. The meanings of lexical items are rooted in their relationships with mind-independent worlds. Two lexical items sharing reference and truth conditions are considered synonymous. To consider two lexical items as non-synonymous, the choice between them depends on a difference in the objects in the external world to which they refer.

Key takeaways

- The external environment is considered as the primary influence on all human speech. The focus is on understanding the relationship between language and the world.
- Meaning is conveyed by the lexical items themselves, without considering context. When defining a lexical item, actual usage is disregarded in favour of prescriptive rules.
- There is a connection between the meaning of a lexical item and the form it takes. The meaning of a lexical item can be understood from its shape or sound. These lexical items are known as onomatopoeic.
- Meaning is resistant to change. The meanings of lexical items are connected to things in the real world, making the process of assigning meanings to lexical items objective.
- Meaning is explained independently of the language user, separate from any individual who speaks or understands the language. Lexical items are objects with inherent properties.

Further reading

Geeraerts (2010) presents an essential and extended account of theories of lexical meaning. Hamawand (2020) examines the contemporary schools of linguistic thought, touching upon the issue of meaning among other things. A brief treatment of many of the historical and contemporary theories of meaning is given in Britannica. Brinton and Brinton (2010) present a helpful summary of Traditional Semantics. Biggs and Geirsson (2020) is a valuable source for understanding the reference theory of meaning. The handbook contains a variety of contributions on several aspects of reference. Saeed (1997) and Abbott (2010) present useful discussions of reference as a theory of meaning. Davidson (1984) provides a clear explanation of the theory of truth conditions. Kamp (1981), Taylor (1998) and McGlone (2012) present further treatments of truth conditions.

References

Abbott, Barbara. 2010. *Reference*. Oxford: Oxford University Press.

Biggs, Stephen and Heimir Geirsson. 2020. *The Routledge Handbook of Linguistic Reference*. New York: Routledge.

Brinton, Laural and Donna Brinton. 2010. *The Linguistic Structure of Modern English*. Amsterdam: Benjamins.

Davidson, Donald. 1984. *Inquiries into Truth and Interpretation*. Oxford: Clarendon Press.

Geeraerts, Dirk. 2010. *Theories of Lexical Semantics*. Oxford: Oxford University Press.

Hamawand, Zeki. 2020. *Modern Schools of Linguistic Thought: A Crash Course*. London: Palgrave.

Kamp, Hans. 1981. A Theory of Truth and Semantic Representation. In Jeroen Groenendijk (ed.), *Formal Methods in the Study of Language*. Amsterdam: University of Amsterdam. 277–322.

McGlone, Michael, 2012. Propositional Structure and Truth Conditions. *Philosophical Studies* 157 (2): 211–25.

Saeed, John. 1997. *Semantics*. London: Blackwell Publishers.

Taylor, Kenneth. 1998. *Truth and Meaning: An Introduction to the Philosophy of Language*. London: Blackwell Publishers.

CHAPTER FIVE

Structural Lexical Semantics

Preview

This chapter explores the basic structural approaches to the study of lexical meaning. The aim is to offer a coherent picture of the different ways of thinking held by structural semanticists about lexical meaning. The chapter is organized as follows. The first section serves as the introduction, reviewing Structural Lexical Semantics and addressing the axioms suggested by prominent scholars in the field that have a profound effect on the analysis of language. The second section presents the fundamental idea underlying the structural paradigm, which is relational. It introduces the dominant strategies proposed by structural semanticists in the study of lexical meaning: lexical fields and sense relations. This section explains in detail how each strategy works in semantic analysis. The third section is a critical appraisal that assesses the proposed strategies to judge their value and relevance. The final section sums up the main points of the chapter.

Introduction

Structural Lexical Semantics is a branch of structural linguistics that originates from the work of the Swiss linguist Ferdinand de Saussure. It is a synchronic study of a language at a specific moment in time. It is a descriptive study of how language is constructed, viewing language as a dual interactive system of symbols and concepts. Language consists of signs with two parts: a signifier (form/substance) and a signified (meaning/concept). The interaction of form and meaning gives rise to language, with an arbitrary relationship between the form of an item and its meaning. Language is a self-contained system where every item gains identity and validity only within the system. Meaning is relational, focusing on the internal elements of the language system. The meaning of an item corresponds to the value it acquires in relation to other items in the language. According to Saussure, each language has its own unique structure governed by internal rules that do not mimic any other language.

Axioms

- A lexical item comprises two components: a signifier and a signified. Both components of the item are inseparable. Like two sides of a piece of paper, one side simply cannot exist without the other. The meaning of lexical items arises from the association of the signifier and the signified, with this association being arbitrary. There is no inherent connection between an item's form and its meaning. The connection is determined by chance, not by principle.

- The meaning of a lexical item is established by its position within a network of semantic relations with other items in the language. Lexical items are organized into semantic or lexical fields, coherent subsets of vocabulary sharing the same conceptual area. These fields are held together by denoting entities in the associative field. Language is an interwoven network in which the lexical items are defined by their relationship to one another.

- Lexical items are defined by two types of sense relations: syntagmatic and paradigmatic. Syntagmatic relations involve lexical items occurring sequentially in speech or writing, as in the relationship between *the, sun, is* and *shining* which are chained together into the sentence *The sun is shining*. Paradigmatic relations involve lexical items that can be substituted for each other in a given context, as in the relationship of the lexical item *sun* in *The sun is shining* to other lexical items such as *moon, star* or *light* that could be substituted for it in the sentence.

Strategies

The fundamental idea underlying Structural Lexical Semantics is the **relational approach**, where the meaning of a lexical item derives from its relation to other lexical items in the language. This means linking one lexical item to another based on semantic grounds. The meaning of a lexical item can be defined as the total set of meaning relations in which it participates, or as the set of relations that the lexical item contracts with other items in the language. What a lexical item means depends in part on its associations with other lexical items. Lexical items not only have meanings, but they also contribute meanings to the utterances in which they occur. The semantic value of a lexical item is determined by its position in a network or its sense of relations with others. These relations play a central role in the semantics of a natural language. The relational approach is crucial for understanding how lexical items are used, and how meanings are conveyed. It illustrates how lexical items are related to one another, and how new lexical items are created in the language.

In terms of the relational approach, meaning is defined by either lexical fields or sense relations.

Lexical fields

One way of defining lexical items is through the use of lexical fields. A lexical field, also known as a semantic field, is a theory of meaning that dates back to Trier in the 1930s. The theory suggests that the vocabulary of a language consists of clusters of interconnected meanings rather than independent items. The vocabulary of a language is not simply a list of independent items, like the entries in a dictionary. Instead, it is organized into fields where lexical items relate to and define each other in various ways. The precise meaning of any lexical item can only be understood by considering it in relation to others. The semantic value of a lexical item is determined by the other items in the field. Each item in the field represents a different semantic value. Knowing one item requires knowledge of the others. The group of items helps identify the network of contrasts within the lexical field. The absence of a lexical item at a specific point in a language's lexical field is referred to as a lexical gap. Examples of lexical fields include *vehicles*, *colours*, *fruits*, *clothing*, *plants* and *vision*, among others.

For instance, the verbs *rob, steal, pilfer, filch* and *purloin* are part of a field denoting *theft*, each with a distinct meaning. *Rob* means 'stealing money or property from a person or place', as in *robbing a bank*. *Steal* means 'taking objects from a person or shop', as in *stealing jewels*. *Pilfer* means 'stealing things of little value or in small quantities, especially from the place where you work', as in *pilfering stamps from work*. *Filch* means 'stealing something small or not very valuable quickly and secretly', as in *filching an apple from the tray*. *Purloin* means 'stealing something or using it without permission', as in *purloining a pen from the office*. These examples illustrate how the lexical items create a conceptual network or mosaic of *theft*. The lexical field in which an item is placed reflects its meaning. The meaning of any lexical item cannot be described in isolation; it is dependent on and contrasts with the meanings of other items in the same lexical field. Any change in the meaning of a single item is connected to a change in related items.

Premises

The lexical field theory is based on focal premises, which can be summarized as follows:

- Language is not a haphazard collection of lexical items. Instead, it is a mosaic of items placed together, where each item occupies a semantic space within the language. The meaning of any item is affected by the other items to which it is related. A lexical item makes no sense outside its field. For example, based on their meanings the lexical items *carve*, *chop*, *crack*, *divide* and *split* cluster together to form the lexical field of breaking or cutting. Each lexical item takes up a position within the field and affects a different entity. People carve wood, chop onions, crack paint or glass, divide money and split cost.

- The lexical items in a field are related to each other directly. The meaning of an individual item is dependent upon the meaning of the rest of the items in the same field. The meaning of an item is internally determined by the set of relations that hold between the item in question and the other items with which it contrasts. Speakers understand a concept by understanding the other concepts that are in the same field. For example, the lexical items *boo*, *cheer*, *groan*, *scream* and *sob* deal with noises made by people in different circumstances. Each lexical item fits a different situation. People cheer in approval, scream in fear, groan in pain, boo in disapproval and sob from sadness.

- The lexical field is exhaustively partitioned among its members; there are no gaps. A lexical gap is a lexical item that does not exist in a language. Each member occupies a certain space within the field. If a single lexical item changes in meaning, then the whole structure of the lexical field changes. If there is an extension in the sense of one lexical item, it narrows the meaning of the neighbouring items. For example, the verbs *murmur*, *mutter* and *whisper* mean to speak softly, but they apply to different circumstances. People murmur when they speak quietly so as not to disturb others, mutter when they grumble in a low voice to themselves, and whisper when they speak so that only one person can hear.

The **lexical field** theory is roughly equivalent to the **dictionary view** of meaning, where a lexical item represents a well-defined bundle of meaning. The core meaning of a lexical item is the information found in its definition. This view aligns with the modularity hypothesis embraced in formal linguistics. The dictionary view is built on several premises. First, there is a distinction between the linguistic (literal) meaning and the non-linguistic (non-literal) meaning of a lexical item. The linguistic meaning of a lexical item consists of context-independent information, while the non-linguistic meaning includes context-dependent information. Based on this premise, it can be inferred that the meaning of a lexical item is separate from its use in language. Secondly, all aspects of meaning contained within a given lexical item are considered equal and structured in terms of positive or negative values. Thirdly, the core meaning of a lexical item is determined by semantics, distinct from the usage of the lexical item which is influenced by pragmatics. Fourthly, knowledge of lexical meaning is independent from cultural, social and physical knowledge. Lastly, the knowledge that a lexical item grants access to is consistent and stored in the mental lexicon.

Practice 5.1

The following lexical items belong to the lexical field of *weakness*. Nevertheless, there exist meaning differences that are overlooked. Can you pinpoint them?

1. frail
2. weak
3. feeble
4. fragile
5. decrepit

Sense relations

Another way of defining lexical items depends on the use of sense relations. Sense refers to the meaning conveyed by a lexical item, while relation is the existing connection between or among lexical items. A sense relation, therefore, is the semantic relationship that exists between the senses of different lexical items within the vocabulary of a given language. It is the semantic link between two or more lexical items within the vocabulary system of a language. The meaning of a language can be understood through the relations between lexical items, where the sense of one lexical item is related to the sense of another. The relation of meaning between lexical items can be on a paradigmatic level as expressed in synonymy and antonymy, or on a syntagmatic level as expressed in anomaly and collocation. The sense of a lexical item can be understood through its similarity with other lexical items or its oppositeness with other lexical items. The sense of a lexical item reveals itself through the relations of meaning that the lexical item forms with other lexical items in the language. Sense relations play an important role in how speakers organize and store the lexical items of their language.

Premises

The sense relation theory is based on several key premises, which can be summarized as follows:

- Sense relations are a matter of inter-lexical relations. The meaning of a lexical item is derived from the meaning of other lexical items. In other words, the lexical items of any language are interrelated to one another and derive their meaning from that relationship. Each item presupposes and defines the other. For example, the two lexical items *pretty* and *attractive* are related to each other, but each has a specific meaning. The lexical item *pretty* means good-looking in an ordinary way but not sexually exciting. By contrast, the lexical item *attractive* means good-looking and sexually exciting. Sense relation is distinct from reference, which relates an item to an entity in the world.

- The dictionary serves as the source of knowledge for the meaning of related lexical items. A dictionary is an alphabetically arranged listing of lexical items in a language that contains information on pronunciation, parts of speech, grammar, definitions, etc. Dictionary knowledge is linguistic. For example, the dictionary entry for the lexical item *car* includes information on pronunciation /ka:/, part of speech (noun), grammar (countable) and meaning (a four-wheeled road vehicle powered by an engine that can carry a small number of people). Synonyms (job, duty, chore) and antonyms (fun, hobby, entertainment) are also provided.

- The structure of the vocabulary of a language can be viewed as a network of different types of sense relations. These relations can be seen through similarity of meaning (synonymy), inclusion of meaning (hyponymy) and opposition of meaning (antonymy). For example, the lexical items *big, small, huge, enormous*, etc. can be grouped together in the semantic field of *size*, with *huge* and *enormous* representing synonymy, and *big* and *small* representing antonymy. Specifically, the lexical item *huge* means very large, whereas the lexical item *enormous* means extremely large, greatly exceeding common size, extent, quantity etc.

Sense relations are of two main types, paradigmatic and syntagmatic. Below is a discussion of each type.

Paradigmatic relations

One way of defining lexical meaning is through a **paradigmatic relation**, which is a pattern of relationship between lexical items that occupy the same position in a linguistic structure. This relation is based on the criterion of **substitution**, which refers to the ability of lexical items to replace each other vertically within a particular context. It determines the choice of one lexical item over another, resulting in different propositions being expressed. Paradigmatic relations operate at all levels of language. For example, in the sound system the phonemes /p/, /l/, and /s/ can all be substituted for /n/ in the context of /-et/. The occurrence of the lexical items of a linguistic structure on a vertical level has some consequences. On the syntactic level, a paradigmatic relation uncovers the speech part of the class to which the selected lexical items belong. For example, in the sentence *It is a small, medium or large size*, the lexical items *small*, *medium* and *large* are all adjectives. On the semantic level, a paradigmatic relation allows lexical items denoting a common concept to be grouped. For example, the lexical items *fit*, *match* and *suit* can be used with clothes, but each lexical item has a specific use. *Fit* is used with size, *match* is used with things and *suit* is used with colour.

The most important paradigmatic relations are antonymy, polysemy, synonymy and taxonomy.

Antonymy

Antonymy is a relationship between two lexical items in which one is the opposite of the other. It is a relationship of incompatibility concerning some given dimension of contrast. The notion of antonymy is derived from the Greek root *anti* which means 'opposite' and denotes opposition in meaning. Antonymy is an important relationship within the vocabulary of a language. Representative examples include *short* x *long*, *asleep* x *awake* and *husband* x *wife*. In some cases, lexical items may have more than one antonym, as in the case of the lexical item *sweet* which has both *bitter* and *sour* as antonyms. The main difference lies in taste or perception. *Bitter* is a strong, sharp, pungent taste that is mostly unlikable, while *sour* is a milder acidic taste that is generally considered pleasant. Antonyms are often divided into primary and marginal types. Primary antonyms are subdivided into three types: gradable, non-gradable and relational.

A **gradable antonym** is a relationship between two lexical items in which the degree of opposition is not absolute. Gradable antonyms typically have a **contrary** relation, with the quality denoted present in varying degrees. These antonyms can be modified by adverbs like *very*, and used in comparative constructions. Examples include *big* x *little*, *clever* x *stupid*, *brave* x *cowardly*, *hot* x *cold*, *polite* x *rude*, and so on. The denial of one lexical item does not imply the assertion of its antonym. For instance, saying *the house is not big* does not mean *it is little*.

A **non-gradable antonym**, also known as **complementary** or **binary**, is a relationship between two lexical items in which the degree of opposition is absolute. Non-gradable antonyms typically have a **contradictory** relation, with the quality denoted not admitting a midpoint. These antonyms cannot be modified by adverbs like *very* or used in comparative constructions. Examples include *open* x *closed, married* x *single, pass* x *fail, hit* x *miss*, and so on. The denial of one implies the assertion of the other. For example, saying something is *dead* means it is *not alive*.

A **relational antonym** is a relationship between two lexical items that are not susceptible to degrees of opposition like gradable antonyms, nor are an either-or matter in character like non-gradable antonyms. Examples include *mother* x *daughter, parent* x *child, plaintiff* x *defendant, murderer* x *victim, father* x *son*, and so on. Relational antonyms exhibit conversibility and reversibility. **Converse antonyms** imply the existence of one when the other exists. Examples include *arrive* x *depart, give* x *take, buy* x *sell, borrow* x *lend, push* x *pull*, and so on. **Reversive antonyms** involve opposition in direction. Examples include *up* x *down, left* x *right, in* x *out, forward* x *backward, in front of* x *behind*, and so on.

Practice 5.2

For each pair of the antonyms below, identify the relationship expressed: gradable, non-gradable, relational, converse or reversive.

1. above x below
2. wide x narrow
3. parent x offspring
4. alive x dead
5. follow x precede

Marginal antonyms can be subdivided into two types: auto-antonyms and anti-antonyms. An **auto-antonym** is a lexical item that has two opposite meanings. These lexical items have multiple meanings, with one being the reverse of another. Context is crucial in avoiding confusion. Here are some examples of lexical items with two opposing meanings.

Bolt	to leave quickly, as in T*he horse bolted when a gun went off.* to fix/immobilize, as in *The bench is bolted to the floor.*
Fast	to move rapidly, as in *You shouldn't drive fast in bad conditions.* to be fixed in place, as in *Tie the boat fast to the pier.*
Consult	to seek advice, as in *If the pain continues, consult your doctor.* to give advice, as in *The man consults for several large companies.*
Bound	to be tied up, as in *Several of the prisoners had been bound.* to be moving, as in *The ship was bound for Italy.*
Temper	to harden, as in *He tempered the steel.* to soften, as in *He tempered his criticism.*

Anti-antonyms are pairs of lexical items that mean the same thing although they look the opposite of each other. For example, both *bone* and *debone* refer to the act of taking the bones out of fish or meat, as in *Ask the fishmonger to bone/debone the fish for you*. In such examples, the prefix reiterates the idea of removal, serving as an intensifier. Other examples include *dehair*, *delouse*, *denude*, *descale*, *deworm*, etc.

Practice 5.3

The following lexical items can have two meanings, one of which is the opposite of the other. Give the meanings.

1. clip
2. dust
3. ravel
4. cleave
5. sanction

Polysemy

Polysemy, also known as **polysemia**, is a language feature in which a lexical item has several meanings. The name comes from the Greek word *poly* meaning 'many' and *semy* meaning 'meaning'. A lexical item, also referred to as a **polyseme**, that has more than one distinct but related meaning, is said to be **polysemous** or **polysemic**. For example, the lexical item *head* displays many meanings. In *She nodded her head*, it refers to an object: part of the body above the neck. In *She sat at the head of the table*, it refers to a location: the beginning or end of something. In *She is a good head taller than her sister*, it refers to a measure: using a person's head as a unit of measurement for size. In *The thought never entered my head*, it refers to an abstract entity: the mind. In *She resigned as head of the department*, it refers to rank: a person who is in charge of a group of people or an organization. In *Their head office is in New York*, it refers to importance: the main office of a company. As can be seen, the multiple senses that the lexical item *head* has are related in some way: the first three are concrete while the last three are abstract. Polysemy contrasts with **monosemy**: a lexical item, usually technical, that has only a single meaning.

Polysemy can also be contrasted with **homonymy**, a relationship between two lexical items that sound alike but differ in meaning, or the relationship between two lexical items that have the same spelling but different meanings. Based on this definition, homonyms are of two types.

Homophony is a relationship between two or more lexical items that are pronounced alike but have different spellings and meanings, as in *some/sum, meat/meet, pale/pail, right/write, sew/so, flour/flower, bare/bear,* and so on. In a dictionary, homophones are usually listed as separate entries. **Homography**, on the other hand, is a relationship between two or more lexical items that are spelled alike but have different meanings and pronunciations, as exemplified in *bow* (to move your head forwards and downwards) /baʊ/ vs. *bow* (a weapon used for shooting arrows) /bəʊ/. Other examples include *wind* (air blowing) /wɪnd/ vs. *wind* (make a clockwork) /waɪnd/, *bass* (tone) /beɪs/ vs. *bass* (fish) /bas/, *tear* (rip) /teə/ vs. *tear* (liquid from the eye) /tɪə/, *refuse* (reject) /rɪˈfjuːz/ vs. *refuse* (waste material) /ˈrefjuːs/, and so on. In a dictionary, homographs are usually listed as separate entries.

Both polysemy and homonymy refer to lexical items having multiple meanings. Polysemy refers to the coexistence of many possible meanings for a lexical item, whereas homonymy refers to the existence of two or more lexical items having the same spelling or pronunciation but different meanings. With polysemy, one form bears two or more related meanings, whereas with homonymy one form bears two or more unrelated meanings. An example of polysemy is the lexical item *good*. In *Her father is a good man*, *good* is used as a moral judgement. In *Her father is a good driver*, *good* is used as a judgement of skill. In both examples, *good* denotes judgement. An example of homonymy is the lexical item *coach*, which refers to either to a person who trains an athlete or a team in sport or to a vehicle for transporting passengers. Although the lexical items share sound and spelling, there is no relation between them. In a dictionary, polysemes are listed under one entry, whereas homonyms are listed under separate entries.

Practice 5.4

The following are polysemous lexical items. For each, give at least three meanings that each conveys.

1. run
2. foot
3. over
4. plain
5. mouth

Synonymy

Synonymy is a relationship between two lexical items in which the meaning of one is similar, but not identical, to the meaning of the other. A lexical item is considered a **synonym** of another item when one of its senses is very similar to the other. For example, the lexical item *collect* is a synonym of the lexical item *pick up* when referring to going somewhere by car to take somebody or something away, as in *I'll collect you/pick you up from the station*. However, they differ in other senses. When talking about collecting things, the lexical item *collect* is used as in *She is collecting coins*. When talking about lifting someone or something from the ground, the lexical item *pick up* is used as in *She picked up the coin lying on the floor*. This shows that total synonymy is difficult to find, as it would mean that lexical items could be substituted for each other in all contexts without a change in meaning. Synonyms are important for expanding lexical choices and avoiding repetitive language use.

Pairs of similar-looking lexical items may share the same conceptual sense but often differ along one or more of the following parameters.

- Dialect. For example, *autumn* is used in Britain, whereas *fall* is used in the United States.

- Style. For example, *begin* is used in informal language, whereas *commence* is used in formal language.

- Connotation. For example, both *hide* and *conceal* mean 'to keep something secret', but they have different connotation. *Hide* may or may not suggest intent as in *He hid the presents in the cupboard*, whereas *conceal* usually implies intent and a refusal to divulge something as in *He concealed the cannabis in the suitcase*.

- Collocation. For example, *high* and *tall* mean 'above the average in height', but they have different collocations. *High* collocates mostly with things that rise from a base like fences, mountains or walls. *Tall* collocates mostly with things that grow high like grass, people or trees. Sometimes, two collocates co-occur with the same lexical item, but the meaning is different. For example, *a little house* has a different meaning from *a small house*. *Little* carries connotations of affection that are absent in the more neutral lexical item *small*.

- Grammatical property. For example, the lexical item *feed* can be used intransitively and transitively, as in *Our kids feed three times a day* and *Let's feed the kids*, while the lexical item *nourish* is used only transitively as in *Fresh food nourishes children*.

Practice 5.5

No two lexical items have exactly the same meaning. Apply this principle to the following pairs and demonstrate how different they are in meaning.

1. wet = moist
2. soft = tender
3. coarse = rough
4. strong = robust
5. tremble = shiver

Taxonomy

Taxonomy, also known as **lexical hierarchy**, is a systematic method of organizing lexical items by arranging them into categories. Each category is structured with ranks, where a general term at the **superordinate** (higher) level includes specific terms at the **subordinate** (lower) level. The superordinate term represents a high level, whereas the subordinate terms provide detailed information and distinctive properties of the category. For example, in the hierarchy *plant–tree–oak* the lexical item *plant* is at the superordinate rank, whereas the lexical item *oak* is at the subordinate rank. Each rank in the hierarchy has a specific level above it.

There are two main types of lexical hierarchy: hyponymy and meronymy, which differ in the nature of the sense relations between lexical items.

Hyponymy

Hyponymy is a type of taxonomy that describes the relation between two lexical items where the meaning of one is included in the meaning of the other. The superordinate item with a general meaning is called a **hypernym**, while the subordinate item with a specific meaning is called a **hyponym**. The relation is described as a *kind of*. For example, *fruit* is a hypernym of *apple* because it is general and superordinate, while *apple* is a hyponym or kind of *fruit* because it is specific and subordinate. *Fruit* is general because it denotes a particular set in which *apple* is a kind. An item is considered a hyponym of another if it contains all the linguistic relevant features of that item. A group of items that share the same superordinate term are referred to as **co-hyponyms**. For example, *apple*, *banana* and *orange* are co-hyponyms of *fruit*.

Practice 5.6

Write three hyponyms for each of the following hypernyms to show the inclusion relation.

1. cook
2. mammal
3. cutlery
4. vehicle
5. crockery

Meronymy

Meronymy, also called **partonymy**, is a type of taxonymy that involves a relationship between two lexical items where the meaning of one represents a part of the meaning of the other. It is a connection between the senses of lexical items, with the item denoting being called the **meronym**, and the item denoting the whole being called the **holonym**. A meronym refers to a part or member of something, and the relationship is indicated by the phrase *part of*. For example, the *nose* is a meronym or part of the *face*, while the *face* is the holonym of the *nose*. Lexical items that name parts of the same whole are called **co-meronyms**. For example, *eye, mouth* and *nose* are co-meronyms of the *face*. Each meronym plays a distinct role in the language. Meronymy can be categorized into necessary and optional types. An example of necessary meronymy is *eye<face*, while an example of optional meronymy is cellar<house.

Practice 5.7

Write three meronyms for each of the following holonyms to demonstrate the part-whole relation.

1. car
2. room
3. house
4. camera
5. computer

Syntagmatic relations

Another way to define lexical meaning is through a **syntagmatic relation**, which is a pattern of relationship between the lexical items of a linguistic structure in a linear order. This relation is based on the criterion of **juxtaposition**, which refers to the ability of lexical items to combine horizontally. Syntagmatic relations between lexical items allow us to understand the co-occurrence restrictions within the same construction. These relations, also known as combinatorial relations, operate at all levels of language. For example, in the sound system the phonemes in the lexical item *net* are arranged to make sense. The sequential combination of lexical items in a construction has implications. On the lexical level, syntagmatic relations help us understand the compatibility of lexical items when combined. For example, we can say *heavy rain*, but not *strong rain*. On the semantic level, syntagmatic relations affect meaning by distinguishing between lexical items that may seem synonymous. For example, both *gain* and *win* can occur with *approval*, but *gain* is used with *advantage* and *win* is used with *game*.

The most important syntagmatic relations include anomaly, collocation, colligation and idiomaticity. These sense relations provide different ways to define the meanings of lexical items.

Anomaly

Anomaly is a relationship in which a lexical item does not match the context in which it is used. The lexical item is not in agreement with the surrounding lexical items that it accompanies. For example, in *a sane chair* the expression is grammatically acceptable because it follows the rules of grammar: determiner + adjective + noun. However, it is semantically anomalous because it violates the rules of usage. It is anomalous because the meanings of the lexical items *sane* and *chair* do not normally go together. The expression simply violates the rules of conventional meaning, and is intuitively rejected by competent speakers of English. As such, anomaly involves the violation of the concept of **selection restrictions**, which are syntactic-semantic restrictions that govern the co-occurrence of lexical items. A lexical item tends to select another lexical item with which it can co-occur. For example, the restriction of the lexical item *sane* to humans, as in *a sane person*, and not to non-humans, as in *a sane chair* is a selection restriction.

A lexical item can be anomalous, i.e., different from what is normal or expected, in two ways: pleonasm and zeugma. **Pleonasm** is the use of a lexical item to emphasize what is clear without it. For example, in *seeing with eyes*, the phrase *with eyes* is redundant because it contributes no extra meaning to the lexical item *see*. Other examples of pleonasm include *a new innovation, a female actress, dental toothache, return back, end result, invited guest*, and so on. **Zeugma** is the use of a lexical item that has to be interpreted in two different ways at the same time to make sense. In *The bread was baking, and so was I*, the lexical item *baking* could refer either to bread being cooked in the oven or to the person getting fed up with waiting. Other examples of zeugma include *She always pays him the money and compliments, He carried the injured and the responsibility for their lives, He was wearing a puzzled look on his face, and a new coat, She could well expire before her club membership does, She held her breath and her father's hand tightly*, and so on.

Practice 5.8

The examples below are syntactically well formed but semantically anomalous. Show how they disregard the constraints on selection.

1. I heard a lion barking.
2. The plant passed away.
3. The engine needs food.
4. The woman drank petrol.
5. Mutton is meat from cow.

Collocation

Collocation, as defined by Sinclair, is a pattern in which a lexical item is typically found. It represents a relationship in which two lexical items occur together in spoken or written language. Collocation is extremely useful in determining the meanings of lexical items in communication. For example, the collocations of *sensual* describe things related to the body, as in *They were moved by the sensual movements of the dancer*, whereas the collocations of *sensuous* describe things related to the mind, as in *They appreciated the sensuous music of the concert*. Therefore, it can be said that *sensual* is a common collocate of movement, whereas *sensuous* is a common collocate of music. This indicates that lexical items typically occur with certain items and less frequently with others. This combination is influenced by the principle of **compatibility**, which is the tendency of lexical items to co-occur in specific positions due to sharing certain syntactic-semantic features. For instance, the verb *do* is compatible with *exercise* as a direct object, but not with *cake*, which typically takes *make*. The adjective *thick* is compatible with both *fog* and *soup*, while only *dense* is compatible with *fog*.

Constructions are of two types: head-complement and head-modifier. The head is the central element in the construction because it determines the semantic character of the whole construction. A complement is an autonomous element that fills a gap in the semantic structure of the dependent head, adding intrinsic conceptual substance to the head. Therefore, a complement like *the door* in *close the door* cannot be omitted. On the other hand, a modifier is a dependent element that has a gap in its semantic structure filled by the head, adding non-intrinsic specifications to the head. Therefore, a modifier like *dangerous* in *a dangerous road* can be omitted without making the construction ungrammatical. The distinction between complements and modifiers has consequences for lexical selections, as heads select their complements, whereas modifiers select their heads. For example, the head verb *boil* selects complements, such as liquids or vegetables like *beans, carrots, potatoes*, and so on. The modifier *utterly* selects heads with negative connotations such as *appalling, exhausted, miserable, nonsensical*, and so on.

The tendency of lexical items to occur together in collocation is known as **collocability or collocational range**. A related term is **semantic prosody**, used in corpus-based lexicology to describe a lexical item that typically co-occurs with other lexical items belonging to a particular semantic set. Collocations are, thus, semantically based, with meaning usually extending from one lexical item to another. Complements that follow heads in a collocation must fall within a particular semantic field. For example, the lexical item *cause* usually collocates with unpleasant things like *difficulty, distress, pain, trouble*, and so on, giving it a negative prosody. In contrast, the lexical item *bring about* collocates with pleasant things like *cure, improvement, solution, success*, and so on, giving it a positive prosody. Therefore, one can say *a problem is caused* and *a solution is brought about*.

Practice 5.9

The following are different patterns of collocation. For each pattern, write the lexical items that complete it.

1. verb + noun
2. noun + noun
3. verb + adverb
4. adjective + noun
5. adverb + adjective
6. noun + verb
7. verb + preposition

Colligation

Colligation is a grammatical pattern in which a lexical item is situated. It shows the position of a lexical item in a sentence and/or limits the types of its complements. In English, adjectives can be used either attributively or predicatively. An **attributive adjective** comes before a noun. For example, the adjective *main* can only be used attributively, as in *the main road*. A **predicative adjective** comes after a verb. For example, the adjective *afraid* can only be used predicatively, as in *the child is afraid*. Some adjectives can be used both attributively and predicatively. For example, in *my old friend*, the adjective *old* is used attributively to describe friendship. It expresses an attribute of the noun. In *my friend is old* the adjective *old* is used predicatively to describe age. It expresses a state of being. The same attributive-predicative distinction applies to the positions of English nouns when they function as modifiers. For example, the noun *paper* can be used attributively, as in *a paper cup*, and predicatively, as in *a cup made of paper*.

Practice 5.10

Some lexical items combine with multiple prepositions. When one preposition is replaced with another, the meaning is completely altered. How?

1. agree on   vs.   agree with
2. arrive at   vs.   arrive in
3. ask about   vs.   ask for
4. happy for   vs.   happy about
5. angry at   vs.   angry with
6. think of   vs.   think about
7. blame for   vs.   blame on
8. throw at   vs.   throw to

9. impact of   vs.   impact on
10. responsible for vs.   responsible to

When it comes to verbs, they can take different types of complements relative to their semantics. For instance, the verb *let* takes the bare infinitive, as in *Let him relax on the beach*. The verb *want* takes the to-infinitive, as in *He wants to relax on the beach*. The verb *enjoy* takes the gerund, as in *He enjoys relaxing on the beach*. Verbs also have specific prepositions they are associated with. For example, the verb *acquit* is colligated with the preposition *of*, forming the phrase *acquit of*, as in *The jury acquitted him of murder*. Adjectives also have specific prepositions they are used with. For example, the adjective *clever* takes the preposition *at*, as in *She's clever at getting what she wants*. Some adjectives can take two prepositions, with a difference in use. For instance, the adjective *anxious* takes *about* with things as in *He seemed anxious about the exam*, and *for* with people as in *Parents are naturally anxious for their children*.

Practice 5.11

Identify the complement that each verb below takes: bare infinitive, to-infinitive or -ing gerund. Then, construct a sentence using the verb and its complement. Some verbs may require two complements.

1. like
2. make
3. recall
4. intend
5. pledge

Idiomaticity

Idiomaticity is the quality of being idiomatic. An idiomatic expression, or **idiom**, is a group of lexical items that have a particular meaning different from the meanings of the items individually. Unlike a collocational phrase, which is mainly compositional, an idiom is non-compositional. Its meaning cannot be derived from the combined meanings of its lexical items. Idioms are stored in the mental lexicon as ready-made forms. For example, the meaning of the idiom *to pull someone's leg* is not based on the meanings of the lexical items *pull* and *leg*. Idiomatically, it means 'to tell someone something that is not true as a way of joking with them'. Unlike a collocational phrase, which can undergo grammatical changes, idioms are grammatically and lexically fixed. No modification or pluralization of any of its lexical items is possible. Idioms often derive their meanings from metaphorical interpretations. For example, in *get/have a handle on something*, the original meaning is 'putting a handle on a physical object that helps to open or carry it', but the metaphorical meaning is 'being able to understand somebody or something so that you can deal with it or them later', as in *I can't get a handle on these sales figures*.

Practice 5.12

The following expressions are considered idioms in English. Can you figure out what each means?

1. sit tight
2. hit the hay
3. give a shot
4. cut corners
5. break the ice
6. keep an eye on
7. draw a longbow
8. make ends meet
9. pull someone's leg
10. Keep your chin up

Critical appraisal

Structural Lexical Semantics is a branch of structural linguistics that focuses on structure of language. It emphasizes synchronic over diachronic analysis. Language is a complex system of relationships, with every lexical item being integrated into the system through a network of relationships. The meaning of a lexical item is relational. It is determined by its position in lexical fields and sense relations. A lexical field is a group of lexical items that contrast with each other in a specific field. A sense relation is a paradigmatic and syntagmatic relation between the lexical items in a language. Although Structural Lexical Semantics provides some insights into lexical meaning, it has some limitations:

- Structural Lexical Semantics does not recognize the role of context in assigning a lexical item to a field. Contrary to this premise, the use of context is crucial, as it provides the best evidence available for the interpretation of an item. A lexical item carries not only a semantic meaning, but also a pragmatic meaning. According to the lexical field theory, the grammatical expressions *quite*, *rather* and *fairly* belong to a field meaning 'comparatively'. However, the structural description lacks contextual details. *Quite* means completely or wholly, as in *The food at the restaurant was quite good; you should go there*. *Rather* means slightly or somewhat, as in *The food was rather good though the restaurant looked ordinary from the outside. Fairly* means nearly or practically, as in *The food was fairly good though we ate better at the other restaurant last night.*

- Structural Lexical Semantics ignores the role of the speaker in conceptualizing the world. One aspect of knowing a lexical item is understanding how that item is used with other items. However, if this is the sole criterion, then the semantic structure of a language becomes a vast calculus of internal relations, disconnected from how speakers conceptualize the world. The use of a lexical item reflects the speaker's intention and responds to the communicative needs of the discourse. In light of lexical field theory, the grammatical expressions *can, may* and *might* denote possibility. However, the structural description lacks conceptual details. *Can* denotes a possibility that is always present, as in *Everyone can make mistakes. May* denotes possibility in a particular case, as in *The cause of the accident may never be discovered. Might* denotes a possibility that is less likely, as in *I might visit you next year if I can save enough money.*

- Structural Lexical Semantics does not draw a sharp distinction between the lexical items within lexical fields, nor does explain the exact differences between them. It fails to consider the contribution made to language by each lexical item. In virtue of the lexical field theory, the grammatical expressions *must, have to, should* or *ought to* suggest obligation or necessity. However, the structural description lacks specific details. *Must* suggests obligation that comes from the speaker, as in *I must take my medicine, otherwise I'd be very ill. Have to* suggests an obligation from an external source, as in *I have to take the medicine, the doctor told me to. Should* and *ought to* suggest obligation in the form of advice that may not be followed, as in *I should or ought to take my medicine, but I often forget. Ought to* is less frequent than *should.*

Therefore, in order to gain a better understanding of lexical meaning, a new theory with the necessary tools is required. This new theory is called Cognitive Lexical Semantics. At the core of this theory, which is the subject matter of Part III, is the belief that language is a fundamental aspect of human cognition. The theory focuses on the relationship between meaning and the mind, viewing meaning as a conceptual construct within the conceptual structure during speech. Meaning plays a crucial role in all linguistic phenomena and is explained through general cognitive strategies, such as prototype, frame, construal, metaphor and metonymy. Grammar and lexicon are seen as interconnected parts of a unified continuum, explained through general cognitive mechanisms. Ultimately, language phenomena are rooted in human experience and events of the world.

Summary

In this chapter, I have provided a brief overview of Structural Lexical Semantics, a theory that examines how the vocabulary of a language is structured. The theory aims to demonstrate that language vocabulary is a cohesive whole where no element operates in isolation. Structural Lexical Semantics introduces two key concepts: lexical fields and sense relations. Lexical fields organize related meanings into sets based on common semantic properties or experiential aspects. Sense relations establish semantic connections between lexical items. These relations are present in the minds of both speakers and listeners during communication. However, Structural Lexical Semantics does not propose any underlying conceptual foundation, leading to a relatively informal and, at times, somewhat vague description.

Key takeaways

- The focus of the theory is laid on the internal structure of language, overlooking the role of language users and the connection between language and the non-linguistic world.
- Language is viewed as a self-contained system where lexical items are interrelated, with their meanings defined by their interactions within the system.
- The theory neglects aspects of meaning that go beyond literal interpretations, leading to a lack of consideration for implied meanings of lexical items.
- The meaning of a lexical item can be understood through its association with a specific field or sense relations, aiding in the comprehension of nuances and variations in meaning.
- Meaning is not an individual experience but rather a product of a shared system of signification arising from interaction with the physical and social world.

Further reading

Introductions to Structural Semantics are provided by Lyons (1963), Coseriu and Geckeler (1981), Greimas (1984) and Matthews (2009). Broad overviews of lexical/semantic field theory are provided by Ohmann (1951), Spence (1961), Lehrer (1974) and Lyons (1977). Detailed discussions of lexical relations are given in Lyons (1977), Cruse (1986), Murphy (2003) and Fellbaum (2014).

References

Coseriu, Eugenio and Horst Geckeler. 1981. *Trends in Structural Semantics*. Tübingen: Narr.

Cruse, Alan. 1986. *Lexical Semantics*. Cambridge: Cambridge University Press.

Fellbaum, Christiane. 2014. Lexical Relations. In John Taylor (ed.), *The Oxford Handbook of the Word*, 350–63. Oxford: Oxford University Press.

Greimas, Algirdas Julien. 1984. *Structural Semantics: An Attempt at a Method*. Nebraska: University of Nebraska Press.

Lehrer, Adrienne. 1974. *Semantic Fields and Lexical Structure*. Amsterdam: North Holland.

Lyons, John. 1963. *Structural Semantics*. Oxford: Blackwell.

Lyons, John. 1977. *Semantics*. Two volumes. Cambridge: Cambridge University Press.

Matthews, Peter. 2009. *A Short History of Structural Linguistics*. Cambridge: Cambridge University Press.

Murphy, Lynne. 2003. *Semantic Relations and the Lexicon: Antonymy, Synonymy, and Other Paradigms*. Cambridge: Cambridge University Press.

Nerlich, Brigitte and David Dana Clarke. 2000. Semantic Fields and Frames: Historical Explorations of the Interface between Language, Action and Cognition. *Journal of Pragmatics* 32: 125–50.

Ohmann, Suzanne. 1951. Theories of the Linguistic Field. *Word* 9: 123–34.

Spence, Nicol C. W. 1961. Linguistic Fields, Conceptual Systems and the Weltbild. *Transactions of the Philological Society* 60 (1): 88–106.

CHAPTER SIX

Generative Lexical Semantics

Preview

This chapter explores the generative approaches to the study of lexical meaning. The aim is to examine the scholarly insights provided by generative semanticists on lexical meaning. The chapter is structured as follows. The first section serves as the introduction, reviewing Generative Lexical Semantics and focusing on the axioms proposed by notable scholars in the field, which are said to have an important influence on the investigation of lexical meaning. The second section presents the core idea of the generative paradigm, which is decompositional. It introduces three different strategies that investigate the topic of lexical meaning: Componential Analysis, Natural Semantic Metalanguage and Conceptual Semantics, explaining in detail how each strategy functions in language analysis. The third section is a critical evaluation of the strategies to assess their quality and validity. The final section summarizes the main points covered in the chapter.

Introduction

Generative Lexical Semantics, also known as formal semantics, is a branch of generative linguistics, developed by Lakoff, McCawley, Postal and Ross in the early 1970s as a response to transformational generative grammar. Generative Lexical Semantics posits two levels of meaning representation. The first level is the deep structure, which is the most fundamental form of an expression that is logical in nature. The second level is the surface structure, which is the form of an expression that is spoken or heard. The deep structure is then transformed into the surface structure through transformational rules. Meaning is analysed using logical systems of analysis, or calculi, making it more similar to mathematics than linguistics. Meaning is decompositional, broken down into an inventory of primitive units of meaning. For example, the meaning of the causative verb *to kill* is decomposed into CAUSE-BECOME-NOT-ALIVE. These primitive units are what ultimately translate into the surface structure, with them being the only ones for surface interpretation. Therefore, all meaning is contained within the deep structure.

Axioms

- The meaning of a lexical item exists outside the mind. This stance is rooted in the **objectivist** theory of meaning, which defines meaning as the correlation between what is expressed and what is observed. This theory emphasizes objective phenomena over subjective experience, as opposed to approaches that define meaning based on communication, use or the speaker's perspective on a situation. For example, the lexical items *wound* and *injury* both refer to the same objective phenomenon: of physical damage to the body, making them interchangeable. However, in terms of subjective experience, they differ. The lexical item *wound* typically results from an intentional action, such as being caused by a weapon, as in *The victim suffered a severe stab wound*. On the other hand, the lexical item *injury* usually results from an accident, like a crash, as in *Several train passengers sustained serious injuries in the crash*.

- The meaning of a lexical item can be described by using mechanical devices. These devices consist of an inventory of the smallest, potentially universal, semantic primitives, inspired by mathematics, computer science or logical work. This stance is rooted in the **formalist** theory of meaning, which utilizes abstract symbols and rules in a quasi-mathematical format to describe language phenomena, including lexical phenomena. For instance, the lexical items *assembler* and *collector* both share the components [human] + [adult] + [± male]. However, their usage differs. The lexical item *assembler* refers to a person who puts together a machine or its parts, as in *The worker is an assembler of electric cars*. On the other hand, the lexical item *collector* refers to a person who gathers things as a hobby like stamps or as a profession like taxes, as in *He earned his living as a tax collector*.

- The meaning of a lexical item is referential. Meaning is found in the relationship between the item and a specific entity in the world. This stance is based on the **denotation** theory of meaning, which defines meaning as the relationship between a lexical item and its referent.

Meaning is closely tied to denotation, where the meaning of a lexical item involves correctly applying it to an object in the world. For example, the lexical items *referee* and *umpire* both refer to a person who ensures that rules are followed in a sports game. However, their usage differs. The lexical item a *referee* typically oversees contact sports like football, basketball and handball, as in *The referee awarded a free kick to the home team*. On the other hand, the lexical item an *umpire* typically officiates non-contact sports games like cricket, tennis and baseball, as in *The umpire penalized the tennis player for yelling*.

Strategies

A predominant tendency in Generative Lexical Semantics, developed by Goodenough and Lounsbury, is the **decompositional** approach. This approach defines the meaning of a lexical item in a given language in terms of semantic components, building meaning from simpler elements. The meaning can be analysed as combinations of a small number of concepts that form structures just as lexical items combine to form sentences. This is consistent with the theory of **atomism** of meaning, where the meaning of a lexical item can be determined in isolation by its semantic components. The definition of a lexical item must include only semantically simpler lexical items. Lexical items are translated into mathematical-type formulas and then subjected to rigorous tests. Within the decomposition technique, there are three models of analysis: componential, natural and conceptual. This theory opposes the structural theory of **holism**, where the meaning of a lexical item is determined by its relations with all other lexical items in the language. In brief, generative theories of meaning are atomistic, whereas structural theories of meaning are typically holistic.

Componential Analysis

One decompositional theory of lexical meaning in Generative Lexical Semantics, developed by Hjelmslev in Europe and Katz and Fodor in America, is **Componential Analysis**. It is a type of definitional analysis in which the meaning of a lexical item is decomposed into a set of smaller units of meaning known as **semantic components** or **semantic features**. These components are lexical items that determine the semantic content of a lexical item. They combine in different ways to form the meaning of individual lexical items. These components are thought to be universal; they are part of the cognitive and perceptual system of the human mind. The analysis is conducted in terms of binary features, which are either present or absent. The use of binary features in semantics (containing only two possible values: + or −) is a logical development from the use of binary features in phonology advanced in the structuralist tradition. Just as phonemes are described using contrastive dimensions such as [± voiced], [± labial] [± nasal], lexical items can be characterized based on oppositions, presented as paired positive and negative features. Every lexical item in the language consists of a unique bundle of semantic features.

Presumptions

- The meaning of a lexical item is a complex semantic structure, defined by a set of minimal components. Within the structure, one component is dominant, around which all others are organized. These components aim to define the lexical item. For instance, the lexical item *stallion* is composed of the semantic components *horse* and *male*. Componential Analysis involves breaking down the meaning of a lexical item into its minimal components, or sense components to understand how lexical meanings are built up compositionally from simpler lexical items.

- The components are used to compare lexical items, distinguishing their meanings and explaining their place within a set. Through Componential Analysis, the difference in meaning can be represented by the presence or absence of a single feature. For instance, the lexical items *chair* and *sofa* both fall under the semantic domain of furniture, sharing features like having a back, legs, and being for sitting. The defining feature that sets them apart is that a *chair* is for one person, while a *sofa* is for two or more people. This allows for a clear contrast between the two lexical items through different definitions.

An example

Lexical items are bundles of meaning components, represented by features. These components show the common and distinguishing meanings of lexical items. For example, consider the lexical items *man* and *woman*. Their meanings are constructed from components such as man [+ human, + adult, + male] and woman [+ human, + adult, − male]. It is evident that both share the components [human] and [adult], but differ by the component [± male]. This indicates that they share all features except one. The information from the Componential Analysis is similar to that found in a definition, and these components cannot be further broken down through semantic analysis. There is a limited and finite inventory of such components. Instead of requiring additional components to define a lexical item, they can be defined by having the same feature with a different value. A plus value signifies the presence of a component in the meaning, whereas a negative value implies its absence.

Practice 6.1

According to the componential conception of meaning, the following nouns share the semantic components: [human] + [adult] + [± male]. Nonetheless, there exist meaning differences that are ignored. Can you diagnose them?

1. juror
2. referee
3. reviewer
4. surveyor
5. arbitrator

Natural Semantic Metalanguage

Another decompositional theory of lexical meaning in Generative Lexical Semantics, initiated by Wierzbicka and colleagues in the 1970s, is **Natural Semantic Metalanguage**. It is a theory of semantics based on the concept that the meaning of a lexical item is defined in terms of a universal set of **semantic primes** or **primitives**. These semantic primitives are utilized to analyse the meanings of lexical items and grammatical categories in a specific language. They form a Natural Semantic Metalanguage and constitute a set of lexical universals, as each primitive has a direct translation in every human language. They are identified by defining lexical items through a process of reductive paraphrasing. The semantic primitives exist as a subset of ordinary natural language, providing the tools to effectively paraphrase the entire vocabulary of any language. The inventory of semantic primitives for defining meaning includes words like I, you, someone, think, know, want, feel, good, bad, big, small, here, there, far, near, much, many, live, die, because, if, maybe, not and more.

Presumptions

- The meaning of a lexical item is defined by a set of semantic primitives that are innate and natural, expressing human concepts. These primitives are universal, present in every language, and are lexicalized in all languages worldwide. They serve as a useful tool for cross-linguistic explanation and include substantives, determiners, quantifiers, evaluators, descriptors, predicates, time, location and more. According to Wierzbicka, the lexical item *sun* can be defined as follows: X was watching Y; for some time X was doing something; because X thought: when something happens in this place, I want to see it; because X was doing this, X could see Y during this time.

- Definitional analysis is characterized as a reductive paraphrase that breaks down meaning into primitive components. It is reductive as it simplifies meaning into these components and is a paraphrase as it provides a textual explanation in simpler, non-technical language. It consists of natural language sentences expressing the meaning of something. For example, Wierzbicka offers a preliminary definition of the lexical item *sun* as follows: something; people can often see this something in the sky; when this something is in the sky; people can see other things because of this; when this something is in the sky; people often feel something because of this.

An example

According to the Natural Semantic Metalanguage, a set of semantically minimal or primitive expressions is used to analyse the meanings of lexical items. This means that the semantics of lexical items can be reduced to a very restricted set of semantic primitives. All aspects of meaning can be described in terms of a small set of primes, all of which can be expressed linguistically. For example, the semantic definition of the lexical item *sky* can be created by using the semantic primitives above and far. The lexical item *sky* can be defined as 'something is very big; people can see it; it is a place; it is above all other objects; and it is far from people'. This example demonstrates how the meaning of the lexical item *sky* is deconstructed into appropriate primes until its core meaning is found. It is evident that the primes represent meanings that exist in the vocabulary of every language. These primes are lexical items of natural language that help interpret the values of other lexical items and identify the structure of thought hidden behind the form of language.

Practice 6.2

According to the Natural Semantic Metalanguage conception of meaning, the following nouns that describe a 'container' have the same semantic primes. However, there exist meaning differences that are missed. Can you determine them?

1. bag
2. box
3. sack
4. packet
5. wallet

Conceptual Semantics

A further decompositional theory of lexical meaning in Generative Lexical Semantics is Conceptual Semantics. Ray Jackendoff is the main pioneer of this approach. In light of this theory, the meaning of an entity is a concept in the speaker's mind. The reference established with the entity in the real world is mediated by a mental image of it. A mental image is a concept. Therefore, the meaning of a lexical item is associated with a concept. The relation between the lexical item and extra-linguistic reality is mediated by a concept, which is how the reality is conceptualized in the speaker's mind. Conceptual Semantics breaks lexical concepts up into semantic categories, which help a person understand lexical items and provide an explanatory semantic representation. These semantic categories include events, states, places, amounts, things and properties, among others. These categories can be described as conceptual parts of speech, forming the semantic content that the item or sentence expresses. The goal is to describe how humans express their understanding of the world using linguistic expressions, and how linguistic utterances are related to human cognition.

Presumptions

- The meaning of a lexical item is defined by a set of mental concepts, which are pictures of reality construed by the speaker's mind. Meaning is an information structure encoded mentally by the speaker, so describing meaning involves describing mental representation. The speaker's conceptualizing activity and physical-perceptive experience play a key role in this process, highlighting a link between conceptualization and sensorial experience. Applied to language, there is an identity between lexical items and the concepts they are associated with, functioning as the locus for the understanding of linguistic utterances in context.

- Meaning is a complex structure built up from basic conceptual elements. To understand meaning, a set of universal semantic primitives are proposed. These primitives have the same translation in every language and are the simplest linguistic concepts. They provide an explanatory semantic representation of things. When applied to language, meaning is compositional, as the meanings of lexical items can be determined from the combination of semantic primes that makes them up. These semantic primes are innately understood by all people and are used to identify lexical meaning and define key properties of lexical items.

An example

In using a lexical item, language speakers do not directly refer to the item itself but rather to its mental representation in the mind. The lexical item is defined by embedding conceptual elements into its arguments. It has a conceptual structure with argument slots that are filled by syntactic complements. For example, let's look at the sentence *Sara went to school*. The semantic analysis of this sentence would be [Event GO ([thing SARA], [Path TO ([Place SCHOOL])])]. Each pair of square brackets represents a concept. The concept of an event is represented by the lexical item *go*, which denotes the movement of an object along a path. The lexical item *go* has two arguments to be filled: an object argument and a path argument. In the sentence, *Sara* fills in the object argument position, whereas *to school* fills in the path argument position. The concept of a thing is represented by the noun *Sara*, denoting a person. The concept of a path is represented by the preposition *to*, denoting a path to a goal. The preposition *to* has an argument which is represented by *school*. The concept of place is represented by *school*, denoting a location.

Practice 6.3

According to the conceptual conception of meaning, the following verbs share the conceptual element of an event, meaning 'to keep away from something'. Despite that, there exist unnoticed meaning differences. Can you establish them?

1. shun
2. avoid
3. evade
4. escape
5. eschew

Critical appraisal

In Generative Lexical Semantics, meaning is generated from a universal deep structure into a language-specific surface structure. The first level of syntactic generation is a deep structure in which various changes (transformations) occur to generate the grammatical surface structure. Semantic representation is universal; the deep structure of any sentence is the same in all languages regardless of syntactic differences. The semantic component of grammar is the base from which all syntactic structures can be derived. The derivation of a sentence is a direct transformational mapping from semantics to surface structure. The syntactic component of grammar is independent of semantics.

The meaning of a lexical item is decompositional, seen as componential, conceptual and primitive. The meaning of a lexical item can be broken down into atomic semantic features or distinctive properties. Although Generative Lexical Semantics offers some useful hints on the topic of lexical meaning, it has not provided an adequate explanation of the topic or a plausible solution for the riddles and cannot account for the contextual flexibility of meaning. It suffers from the following limitations.

- In the Componential Analysis model, the focus is on propositional meaning. A proposition is the meaning of a linguistic expression that makes a statement about some state of affairs. The same proposition can be expressed by different linguistic structures. It works best with sets of concrete objects. Thus, it is of more doubtful value in describing the meanings of more abstract items. It excludes non-propositional meaning including descriptive, expressive and social ones. For example, the lexical items *false* and *untrue* share the same proposition: lack of veracity. However, there is a difference in usage that the theory ignores. The former as in *She was charged with giving false evidence in court* is more disapproving than the latter as in *Their story was completely untrue*. Unlike untrue, the non-propositional content of *false* includes the notion of deliberateness.

- In the Natural Semantic Metalanguage model, lexical items occurring in the same position are considered free alternatives and thus synonymous. As a result, the explanations regarding the relations between lexical items are vague, imprecise and inaccurate. For example, the lexical items *empathy* and *sympathy* can be used interchangeably. Although they express deep feelings, there is a difference in usage that the theory neglects. The lexical item *empathy* is used when one understands the feelings of another but does not necessarily share them, as in *They expressed empathy for other people's situations*. One just feels what another person feels. The lexical item *sympathy* is used when one shares the feelings of another, as in *Our heartfelt sympathy goes out to the victims of the war*. One feels bad for another person's sadness, or one's thoughts are in line with someone else's.

- In the Conceptual Semantics model, the linguistic analyses are carried out in logical terms or mathematical rules. In doing so, it neglects minute distinctions between seemingly similar expressions. It is unable to account for the meaning of other lexical classes than verbs. Although it claims to be universal, it was applied only to English. For example, the lexical items *accident* and *incident* refer to an event. Although both denote events, there is a difference in their spheres of usage that the theory disregards. The lexical item *accident* refers to an event that is bad, unfortunate, unintentional and unplanned, which can cause a major loss to the individuals involved as in *The tourist died following a road accident.* The lexical item *incident* refers to an event that is bad or good, intentional or unintentional, planned or unplanned, as in *It was a small incident involving a cow.*

Due to these limitations, Generative Lexical Semantics is no longer a viable solution to semantic problems. This situation has led to the emergence of a new theory of meaning, called Cognitive Lexical Semantics. According to the cognitive theory of Lexical Semantics, discussed in Part III, it is not feasible to define meaning solely in terms of mechanical devices, without considering the brain or mind. Therefore, formal logic is not sufficient as a theory of natural language semantics. These limitations ultimately led to the demise of Generative Lexical Semantics, which made unfounded assumptions about meaning being governed by formal mechanisms found in mathematical logic. In Cognitive Lexical Semantics, the meaning of lexical items is encyclopaedic: everything known about a lexical item contributes to its meaning. This implies that there is no fundamental distinction between semantics and pragmatics. Semantics encompasses linguistic knowledge, while pragmatics includes world knowledge. Meaning is thus rooted in human experience of the world. Cognitive Lexical Semantics highlights the creative role of speakers in constructing meaning through cognitive abilities, which are grounded in various patterns of perceptual interactions and bodily actions.

Summary

In this chapter, I have presented a brief overview of the theoretical framework of Generative Lexical Semantics, a theory that identifies semantic interpretation directly at the deep structure level. Generative Lexical Semantics has made important contributions to lexical meaning through Componential Analysis, Natural Semantic Metalanguage and Conceptual Semantics. Componential Analysis breaks down the meanings of lexical items into smaller units of meaning called semantic components or features. For example, the meaning of *woman* consists of the components [FEMALE, HUMAN, ADULT]. Natural Semantic Metalanguage reduces the meanings of lexical items to a set of universal semantic primitives. For example, the meaning of the past tense verb *broke* can be described as follows: X broke Y =X did something to thing Y because of this, something happened to Y at this time because of this, after this Y was not one thing anymore. Conceptual Semantics represents the meanings of lexical items as conceptual elements in the mind of an individual language user. For example, the meaning of the sentence *Linda entered the class* can be represented as [EVENT ENTER ([THING Linda], [PATH TO ([PLACE IN ([THING the class])])]).

Key takeaways

- Meaning is derived through a decomposition process, breaking down a lexical item into its minimal components that provide delicate, subtle details of its meaning.

- Meaning resides in the deep structure, capturing the core meaning of a lexical item. From the deep structure, the surface structure is derived through transformation.

- Meaning is dynamic, not a static property. It emerges through the transformation of the deep structure into the surface structure, with form determined by meaning.

- Meaning is a complex abstraction resulting from the interaction between lexical items and conceptual representations, aiding in the generation and interpretation of meaning.

- Meaning is amenable to algorithmic characterization, studied in isolation from cognitive considerations and described without essential reference to cognitive processing.

Further reading

Introductions to semantics in generative grammar are Fodor (1977), Chomsky (1996) and Haim and Kratzer (1998). Advanced introductions to Componential Analysis are Burling (1964), Nida (1979). Readable introductions to Natural Semantic Metalanguage are Wierzbick (1996), Goddard (1998) and Sadow and Mullan (2019), readers in Conceptual Semantics are Jackendoff (1990), Levin and Pinker (1992) and Deane (1996).

References

Burling, Robbins. 1964. Cognition and Componential Analysis. *American Anthropologist New Series* 66 (1): 20–28.

Chomsky, Noam. 1996. *Studies on Semantics in Generative Grammar*. Berlin: de Gruyter.

Deane, Paul. 1996. On Jackendoff's Conceptual Semantics. *Cognitive Linguistics* 7 (1), 35–91. Berlin: De Gruyter.

Fodor, Janet. 1977. *Semantics: Theories of Meaning in Generative Grammar*. Hassocks, England: Harvester Press.

Goddard, Cliff. 1998. *Semantic Analysis: A Practical Introduction*. Oxford: Oxford University Press.

Goodenough, Ward H. 1956. Componential Analysis and the Study of Meaning. *Language* 32: 195–216.
Haim, Irene and Angelika Kratzer. 1998. *Semantics in Generative Grammar*. Malden, MA: Blackwell.
Hjelmslev, Louis. 1961. *Prolegomena to a Theory of Language*. Madison: University of Wisconsin Press.
Jackendoff, Ray. 1990. *Semantic Structures*. Cambridge, MA: MIT Press.
Katz, Jerrold J., and Jerry A. Fodor. 1963. The Structure of a Semantic Theory. *Language* 39 (2): 170–210.
Levin, Beth and Steven Pinker. 1992. *Lexical and Conceptual Semantics*. Blackwell.
Nida, Eugene. 1979. *A Componential Analysis of Meaning*. Berlin: de Gruyter.
Sadow, Lauren and Kerry Mullan. 2019. *A Brief Introduction to the Natural Semantic Metalanguage Approach*. Singapore: Springer.
Wierzbick, Anna. 1996. *Semantics: Primes and Universals*. Oxford: Oxford University Press.

PART THREE

Cognitive Lexical Semantics

In this part, I will examine the role that lexical meaning plays inside Cognitive Lexical Semantics. The goal is to identify the tools used to define meaning. This part consists of seven chapters. Chapter 7 delves into the importance of prototypes in explaining the multiple senses of individual lexical items. In this theory, the meaning of a lexical item is understood by referring to a highly typical example. Chapter 8 explores the value of frames in defining the meanings of lexical items as groups. In this theory, the meaning of a lexical item is understood in relation to the frame it activates. Chapter 9 considers the importance of construal dimensions in choosing between different expressions. In this theory, the meaning of a lexical item is determined by the construal imposed on a situation. Chapter 10 examines the role of metaphor in shaping lexical meaning. In this theory, the meaning of a lexical item is based on similarity: comparing one thing to another. Chapter 11 sheds light on the import of metonymy in shaping lexical meaning. In this theory, the meaning of a lexical item is based on contiguity: a part or attribute of a thing represents the thing itself. Chapter 12 looks at the significance of blending in creating lexical meaning. In this theory, the meaning of a lexical item results from integrating or merging parts of linguistic elements. Chapter 13 applies the usage-based theory to the characterization of lexical meaning.

Cognitive Lexical Semantics emerged in the 1980s as a subfield of **Cognitive Semantics**, which is associated with the works of linguists such as Langacker, Lakoff, Fillmore and others. Cognitive Semantic, in turn, is a subfield of **Cognitive Linguistics**, a movement that challenges the generativist view of language. Cognitive Lexical Semantics focuses on the cognitive aspects of language, and how language relates to meaning and cognition. Language is a part of human cognition, and can only describe the world as individuals imagine it. Language is directly related to mental representations, and through them, to the world outside of language. Linguistic patterns reflect fundamental properties of the human mind, and linguistic abilities are inseparable from other cognitive abilities. In Cognitive Lexical Semantics, the meaning of a lexical item refers to a concept in the mind of the speaker that is grounded in perception and experience. The meaning of a lexical item encompasses vast repositories of knowledge, both linguistic and non-linguistic, and serves as a prompt for a variety of conceptual operations. The theory focuses on actual patterns of usage.

Cognitive Linguistics

Cognitive Linguistics is a modern school of linguistics that has grown since the 1970s. It includes a range of approaches that share some common assumptions. Cognitive Linguistics views language as a tool for organizing, processing and conveying information, with all language structures serving this function. It explains language creation, learning and usage by referencing concepts formed in the mind, linking descriptions of linguistic patterns to mental processes. The field places significant emphasis on meaning, which is grounded in experience and explained through human cognition. The meaning of a linguistic expression is derived from perception and cognition, representing a particular way of conceiving a given situation. Linguistic structures encode different ways of perceiving a situation, and vary based on communicative needs.

Cognitive Lexical Semantics adopts fundamental assumptions of Cognitive Linguistics that apply to lexical meaning.

- Language is non-modular. This means that there is no autonomous portion of the brain specialized for language. Externally, language is influenced by general cognitive abilities like perception, memory, reasoning etc. Internally, language interacts with aspects like morphology, phonology, pragmatics, syntax and semantics. An example of non-modularity in language is the interface between semantics and pragmatics. Lexical items can have different meanings depending on context. The lexical item *bachelor* has a semantic meaning of *unmarried man*, but it can also have pragmatic implications such as *eligible for marriage* or not *interested in marriage* depending on the context. This shows that lexical items are explained by simultaneously taking into account other aspects of language. This view contradicts the generative claim of modularity, which holds that the human mind consists of different modules, one of which is language. Each module functions separately from the others.

- Language is symbolic. This means that language uses symbols to stand in for something else based on conventions, not on natural connections. Symbolic language can express ideas, objects or events that are not directly observable. Language is a structured inventory of linguistic units defined as form-meaning pairings. Language provides its speakers with a set of resources for associating phonological structures with semantic structures. For example, the lexical item *rainbow* symbolizes hope and promise, and *red rose* symbolizes love and romance. The association is motivated by the manner in which speakers interact with the world. Accordingly, form cannot be investigated independently of meaning. Form and meaning are seen as mutually interdependent. This view is quite different from the generative claim that there is no direct link between the form of language and the meaning it expresses. So, forms of linguistic expressions are studied separately from their meanings.

- Language is usage-based. This means that language is shaped by how people use it in communication. The meaning of a lexical item is not fixed or innate, but rather depends on the context and the speaker's experience and intention. Language is an embodied and social human behaviour influenced by cognitive processes involved in language use. Language use, therefor, determines language knowledge. For example, the adjective *anxious* can mean *worried* or *eager* depending on the context in which it is used. This view stands in stark contrast to the generative claim that draws a distinction between knowledge of language and use of language. Every human is equipped with a language faculty, an innate cognitive subsystem, which gives rise to competence, unconscious knowledge of language. Knowledge of language arises from what is innate in the mind at birth. This view, referred to as nativism, states that language knowledge (competence) determines language use (performance).

- Language is meaningful. This means that it reflects how speakers experience the world. Therefore, all language elements have meanings and are never empty. Linguistic expressions, whether closed-class or open-class, are inherently meaningful. Language is meaningful because it is based on the idea that grammar is wholly symbolic and that linguistic units are pairings of form and meaning. For example, the lexical item *pen* has a phonological pole (the sound or spelling of the item) and a semantic pole (the concept of a writing instrument) that are linked by a symbolic relation. This symbolic relation is the basis of all linguistic structures. Language is meaningful because grammar forms a continuum with lexicon, and both are based on symbolic structures that pair sounds and concepts. This view contrasts with the generative claim that there are elements in language that are semantically empty. Their presence in linguistic expressions serves only syntactic or morphological functions.

- Language is creative. This means that language is not a fixed system of rules, but a dynamic and flexible tool for expressing meaning and constructing reality. Linguistic creativity is the ability to use language in novel and unexpected ways to create various effects. It is the ability to perceive the world in new ways, to find hidden patterns and to make connections between seemingly unrelated phenomena. It is the act of turning novel and imaginative ideas into reality, or producing or using original and unusual ideas. For example, the speaker has the ability to blend elements from different frames of reference into a new and coherent whole. The expression *couch potato* blends the concepts of a sofa and a vegetable to create a metaphor for a lazy person. This view goes against the generative claim that creativity refers to the ability of humans to generate and understand an infinite number of well-formed sentences in a language by means of a finite set of grammatical rules.

Cognitive Semantics

Cognitive Semantics is a unique theory of meaning, exemplified by linguists like Langacker, Fillmore, Talmy, Lakoff and Fauconnier. It draws ideas from cognitive psychology, anthropology and other fields identifying meaning with conceptualization. This theory views a linguistic expression as encoding a specific way of conceptualizing a situation, with meaning arising from the interaction between expression and human knowledge. A key aspect of the theory is its focus on the subjective nature of meaning, highlighting the speaker's role in construing a situation, determining its meaning, and using language to express it. The theory suggests that the meaning of a linguistic expression relates to a concept in the speaker's mind, grounded in bodily, physical, social and cultural experiences.

Cognitive Lexical Semantics adopts foundational assumptions and methods of Cognitive Semantics that apply to lexical meaning.

Assumptions

Cognitive Lexical Semantics is founded on fundamental assumptions that allow for a fruitful discussion of lexical meaning.

- Meaning is embodied. Linguistic meaning is not abstract, but based on our bodily experiences and interactions with the world. Our understanding of language is shaped by our physical, sensory and emotional experiences. For example, the lexical item *up* is often associated with positive emotions, while the lexical item *down* is often associated with negative emotions. These meanings reflect the embodied nature of language; they are derived from our physical experiences of moving up and down, which in turn shapes our understanding and usage of these lexical items. In Cognitive Semantics, these bodily experiences and interactions with the world play a paramount role in shaping the meaning of linguistic expressions.

- Meaning is motivated. Linguistic forms are driven by cognitive and communicative needs, rather than formal rules. Meaning is not arbitrary or fixed, but rather shaped by various factors such as cognition, experience, culture and context. For instance, the use of the definite article *the* in English is motivated by the speaker's intention to convey a specific referent in context. Similarly, word order in a sentence is often motivated by the speaker's emphasis on certain elements or the discourse context. In Cognitive Semantics, language structure and meaning are closely intertwined, and that these structures often reflect cognitive and communicative goals. Motivation is the non-arbitrary relation between form and meaning.

- Meaning is dynamic. Meaning is not fixed or static but evolves based on cognitive processes and situational contexts. This means that the meaning of a lexical item can evolve and adapt based on the specific circumstances in which it is used. For example, the lexical item *head* can mean both a body part and a leader of a group. This is not a random coincidence, but a result of metonymic thinking, where one thing stands for another thing that is related to it. The *head* is the most prominent part of the body, and the *leader* is the most prominent member of the group, so we use the same item to refer to both concepts. In Cognitive Semantics, meaning is viewed as residing in conceptualization, which is a dynamic activity that changes over time and depends on the context.

- Meaning is encyclopaedic. Meaning includes all knowledge and associations that a speaker has with a lexical item, not just the core or dictionary definition. Understanding a lexical item involves drawing upon a broad array of knowledge that is inherently linked to it. For example, the lexical item *apple* does not just mean a round fruit, but it also brings to mind associations like its taste, texture, colour, origin, use, significance, and so on. This way of understanding meaning is based on the idea that language is conceptualization, showing that it reflects how we perceive and construe reality. In Cognitive Semantics, meaning is encyclopaedic because it is based on our conceptual knowledge of the world and how we conceptualize situations in different ways.

- Meaning is conceptualized. Linguistic units symbolize conceptualizations. They are tied to our understanding of the world. Conceptualization is the process of creating and organizing mental representations of reality. For example, the expression *kick the bucket* conceptualizes death as a sudden and irreversible event. It is not a literal description of what happens when someone dies, but a metaphorical way of talking about death as a physical action. The metaphor is based on an old custom of hanging oneself by standing on a bucket and then kicking it away. In Cognitive Semantics, meaning is the mental activity of conceptualizing a situation in a certain way. Meaning is conceptualized as the mental representation of linguistic symbols and their relations.

Methods

Cognitive Lexical Semantics uses efficient methods that enable a thorough analysis of lexical meaning.

- A lexical item consists of a category of interrelated senses. The category of a given lexical item is a network of distinct but related senses. One sense, known as the prototypical sense, serves as an ideal example from which other senses, known as the peripheral senses, are derived through semantic extensions. The senses are related to each other like members of a family, sharing some general properties but differing in specific details. For example, the prototype of the lexical item *foot* refers to the lowest part of the leg, as in *What size foot do you have?* Peripherally, it refers to the bottom of something, as in *There is a note at the foot of the page*, and a measure of length, as in *She is five feet two inches tall*. This demonstrates that most lexical items are polysemous. Lexical meanings are multifaceted and flexible, meaning they can vary depending on the context of use.

- Lexical items do not exist in isolation but tend to cluster together in frames. Therefore the meaning of a lexical item can be understood as dependent on the frame with which it is associated. A **frame** is a knowledge configuration used to describe the meanings of lexical items. Each item represents a different aspect. An aspect is a portion of a frame associated with a particular concept. To understand the meaning of an item, it is necessary to compare it with other items in the same frame. For example, the meaning of the lexical item *fit* can only be characterized within the frame of clothing, which includes other lexical items like *match* and *suit*. The lexical item *match* refers to colour and appearance. The lexical item *fit* refers to size. The lexical item *suit* refers to style. Each item in this frame carries its own subtle message.

- Lexical items embody alternative construal dimensions of content. The meaning of a lexical item is identified in terms of both conceptual content and construal. Conceptual content is the property inherent in a situation, while construal is the speaker's ability to conceptualize a situation differently and use different lexical items to represent them. Two lexical items may share the same content, but differ in terms of how the speaker construes their common content. For example, the lexical items *jealous* and *envious* both mean feeling unhappy because one wishes one had the advantage somebody else has. Yet, they construe the situation differently. *Jealous* means feeling hostile towards someone who enjoys an advantage, while *envious* means wishing to have the advantage that someone else has. As can be seen, alternative conceptual choices result in different lexical items.

- Lexical meaning is viewed as a reflection of conceptual structure, the concept in the conceptual system that represents the experienced thing. Conceptual structures are the means by which human cognition organizes conceptual content in language, rooted in physical and social experiences. They are aspects of meaning construction in language, grounded in experience and serve to shape the forms of our linguistic expressions, and are crucial in metaphor, metonymy and blending. These allow language users to conceptualize experiences, create new linguistic expressions and account for their interpretations. For example, the blend *transistor* combines *transfer* and *resistor* to create a device that amplifies or switches electrical signals.

- A difference in form always indicates a difference in meaning. Lexical variation is not arbitrary; variants typically have subtle differences in meaning. Each lexical item corresponds to a distinct meaning, with its own semantic content that conditions its presence in a construction. The lexical organization of an item reflects its semantic organization. Language speakers do not accept two lexical items as true synonyms. Every two forms contrast in meaning. When language provides two similar lexical items, speakers try to find a way to distinguish between them. For example, *scream* and *shout* both involve uttering a loud cry, but they are not synonymous. *Scream* involves making a loud sound in moments of fear or pain, while *shout* involves making a loud sound to attract attention or give instructions. Shouting can be either angry or joyful.

The key idea underlying Cognitive Lexical Semantics is the **representational** approach, where the meaning of a lexical item is linked to a specific mental representation, called a **concept**. Concepts are derived from percepts. The connection between a lexical item and its referent is therefore indirect in the mind of the speaker. The meaning of a lexical item reflects not only the content of a conceived situation but also how that content is construed by the speaker. This perspective stems from the subjectivist theory of meaning, which highlights the significance of personal experiences in shaping the representation of lexical items. It acknowledges the speaker's ability to construe a situation in various ways. The subjectivist theory posits that knowledge is influenced by subjective experience, limited to the conscious self and its sensory states. In this sense, it is opposed to objectivism, which asserts that reality is entirely objective and exists independently of the mind.

Cognitive linguists believe that language mirrors the **conceptual system**, which encompasses the concepts available to an individual. The conceptual system embodies our understanding of the world. When a speaker encounters a thing, the thing activates the conceptual system. Within this system, the thing takes a conceptual structure, representing the concept in the conceptual system that corresponds to the experience. This **conceptual structure** is encoded as a **semantic structure** in language, expressed through linguistic form. Therefore, the semantic structure mirrors the conceptual structure, which is encyclopaedic in nature. In an **encyclopaedic view**, a lexical concept serves as a gateway to extensive knowledge repositories. This is quite the opposite of the **dictionary view**, where a lexical concept is a predefined bundle of meaning found in a language dictionary. Ultimately, the construction of meaning is fundamentally conceptual and not inherently linguistic. Meaning is derived from conceptual structures that reflect human experience of the world. These conceptual structures are represented through various cross-domain mappings like metaphor, metonymy and blending.

Outline

A   Cognitive processes 97

7   The prototype theory 99
Introduction 99
Prototype 100
Theses 101
Consequences 102
Critical appraisal 104
Summary 105
Key takeaways 106
Further reading 106
References 106

8   The frame semantics theory 109
Introduction 109
Frame semantics 110
Assumptions 111
Repercussions 112
Critical appraisal 114
Summary 115
Key takeaways 116
Further reading 116
References 117

9   The construal theory 119
Introduction 119
Construal 120
Axioms 120
Ramifications 121
Dimensions of construal 122
Critical appraisal 129
Summary 131
Key takeaways 131
Further reading 131
References 132

B Conceptual mappings 133

10 The conceptual metaphor theory 135
Introduction 135
Metaphor 136
Principles 136
Patterns 138
Advantages 141
Summary 142
Key takeaways 142
Further reading 143
References 143

11 The conceptual metonymy theory 145
Introduction 145
Metonymy 146
Principles 146
Patterns 148
Advantages 150
Summary 151
Key takeaways 151
Further reading 152
References 152

12 The conceptual blending theory 153
Introduction 153
Blending 154
Principles 154
Patterns 156
Advantages 158
Summary 158
Key takeaways 159
Further reading 159
References 159

C Usage mechanisms 161

13 The usage-based theory 163
Introduction 163
Usage-based theory 164

Claims 164
Applications 166
Advantages 169
Summary 170
Key takeaways 171
Further reading 171
References 171

A

Cognitive processes

Cognitive processes are mental operations which the brain performs to process meaning. They are functions of the brain in constructing and interpreting linguistic expressions. Cognitive Linguistics considers language as an integral part of cognition, and a product of general cognitive processes. Cognitive linguists are interested in how language is organized in the mind. They aim to describe how the language faculty of the mind works. They try to find out what cognitive processes are involved in the production and comprehension of language. Cognitive processes enable language users to perform tasks like categorization, configuration and conceptualization, among others. **Categorization** refers to the mental act of grouping together the numerous senses of a given lexical item into a category. A **category** is a network of the senses of a lexical item which is structured in terms of prototype and periphery. **Configuration** refers to the mental act of assembling a number of lexical items into a semantic frame, in which each occupies a specific facet. A **frame** is a coherent area of conceptualization which provides the basis for the characterization of a lexical item. **Conceptualization** refers to the mental act of construing a situation in different ways. **Construal** is the ability to conceive a situation in alternate ways and express them in language by using different lexical items.

Characteristics

- Language is grounded in cognitive processes, rather than abstract ones. They are the same as other cognitive abilities like vision, attention, reasoning, and so on. Language is not an autonomous linguistic faculty emerging from a specific language-acquisition module of the mind.

- Cognitive processes are not linguistic in themselves. They are essential cognitive prerequisites for language use. They are strategies that enable language users to create and express their language. It is on the basis of these cognitive processes that the language system is developed.

- Cognitive processes help conceptualize the experience in different ways, depending on the language user's choices. Each cognitive process is associated with a different kind of communication. For example, focusing allows language users to pay attention to one particular part of a linguistic expression.

- Cognitive processes are involved in the construction of linguistic meaning. Meaning does not reside in objective reality. Rather, it is sought in the realm of cognitive processing. Linguistic structures arise from use events through basic cognitive processes.

- Linguistic alternatives are a reflection of cognitive processes in the human brain. The choice of alternatives depends on the nature of the context in which they are used. Alternations in form spell alternations in meaning. Each alternative has a special discourse function.

CHAPTER SEVEN

The prototype theory

Preview

This chapter explores the role of categorization in the semantic description of individual lexical items. **Categorization** refers to the mental act of grouping the multiple senses of a lexical item into a category. A **category** then is a network of distinct but related senses of a given lexical item. The aim is to identify the key elements of a linguistic item. The chapter is structured as follows. The first section serves as the introduction. It discusses two opposing theories of categorization. The **classical** theory defines categorization in terms of defining features, while the **prototype** theory defines it in terms of degrees of similarity to a central example. The second section introduces the prototype theory of categorization. The third section outlines the main ideas of the theory. The fourth section discusses the implications of the theory for lexical meaning. The fifth section provides a critical evaluation of the prototype theory, assessing its validity and enumerating its advantages. The final section recaps the core concepts of the chapter.

Introduction

An intriguing aspect of the lexicon is **polysemy**, where a linguistic item, whether lexical or grammatical, can have multiple meanings. Most theories acknowledge the existence of various senses for a given item, but they differ in how these senses are organized. The main question is: how are the senses of a lexical item categorized? To answer this question, linguists from different theoretical backgrounds have developed two theories: classical and prototype. Both theories are viewed as essential for understanding experience, but they diverge in their approaches to categorization. These differences stem from their underlying assumptions. The **classical** theory, influenced by philosophy and logic, links meaning to truth conditions and defines meanings in terms of features. In contrast, the **prototype** theory, influenced by psychology, associates meaning with mental representations or bodily experiences and defines meanings in terms of networks. The classical theory places regular senses within a category and excludes the irregular ones, whereas the prototype theory includes all regular and irregular senses in the category.

Prototype

Cognitive Lexical Semantics argues that the meanings of lexical items cannot be defined by abstract semantic features. Instead, they are seen as forming categories with central prototypes and peripheral members. According to the prototype theory, as exemplified in Rosch's work in the 1970s, a category is centred on **a prototype**, which represents the key attributes of the category. This prototype is the most typical example of the category, based on its defining features. Other members that share some, but not all, attributes are considered the **periphery**. Members of a category are not equal. Their inclusion is based on their resemblance to the prototype. While they may differ in some attributes, they are still included in the category due to perceived similarities to the prototype. This theory contrasts with the classical theory of categorization, which requires entities to meet all necessary and sufficient conditions to be part of the category.

To illustrate, consider the category *fruit*. According to the prototype theory, this category is not defined by objective features but by approximations that include prototypical and peripheral members. Prototypical members, such as *apples* and *pears*, have all the attributes of the category (sweet, soft and with seeds). Peripheral members, like *lemons, avocados* and *bananas*, only share some attributes. *Lemons* are peripheral because they are not sweet, *avocados* because they are not soft and *bananas* because they lack seeds. Despite not having all attributes, they are still part of the category. This demonstrates that category members do not have equal status, boundaries can be ambiguous and some members are better examples than others. This complexity makes it challenging to find a single definition that fully captures a category.

Practice 7.1

The lexical items listed below are names of categories. Each category has several members. Write what the members are.

1. boat
2. food

3. sports
4. hobbies
5. clothing

Theses

The prototypical view of categorization is based on key theses, which can be summarized as follows:

- Categories are defined disjunctively. They are not defined by a set of essential attributes that members of a category are expected to manifest. Some of the allegedly essential attributes of the central exemplar of a category may appear to be optional at the periphery. Within a prototypically organized category, membership is based on similarity rather than identity. Let us examine the category *bird*. All types of bird are included in the category. The order in which the types appear hinges on the degree of resemblance of a type to the prototype. The more attributes a type shares with the prototype, the less distant it is. The fewer attributes a type shares with the prototype, the more distant it is.

- Categories display different degrees of salience. Members of a category have different statuses. Attributes not shared by all the members of a category are less important than attributes that appear in all or most of the members. Members of a category that carry more weight are considered better exemplars than members that are less salient. Continuing with the category *bird*, both a *sparrow* and an *ostrich* are types of bird. However, there is a difference in status. A *sparrow* would be a more typical example of bird, whereas an *ostrich* would not because of its inability to fly. Despite this atypical attribute, an *ostrich* would be included as a member of the category.

- Categories have vague boundaries. Categories contain peripheral zones around clear centres. Categories may have marginal instantiations that do not conform rigidly to the central cases. A category is structured in terms of similarity and distance. The more similar a sense is to the centre, the closer in distance it is. The less similar a sense is to the centre, the farther in distance it is. Proceeding with the category *bird*, because the boundaries of the category are vague, all types of bird are included in the category. Because the category is not defined by a single set of attributes, the kind of birdiness that is relevant for sparrow is different from the one for ostrich. Being able to fly is not part of the birdiness of ostrich.

- Categories are flexible. Category membership is defined by similarity rather than identity. The distinction between essential and accidental attributes is not rigid. There need not be a set of attributes that applies to all the members of a category. Category membership is not a question of either-or, but a matter of degree. Therefore, not every member is equally representative of a category. Remaining with the category *bird*, a *sparrow*, and an *ostrich* are both types of bird. Because a sparrow can fly, it is prototypical. Because an ostrich, by contrast, is unable to fly, it is not prototypical. Accordingly, both are members of the category but to different degrees.

Practice 7.2

Consider the category of CHAIR. First, list the attributes that it possesses. Secondly, identify the prototype. Thirdly, rank the remaining examples based on their closeness to the prototype.

rocking chair, swivel chair, kitchen chair, armchair, wheelchair, highchair

Consequences

The adoption of the prototype model of categorization in the description of lexical items has the following pivotal consequences.

- Lexical meaning is subjective. The meaning of a lexical item is subjective in the sense that it arises from real-world scenarios and user-specific background data. This view is influenced by the theory of **subjectivism** or **experientialism**, which suggests that symbols used in a language derive their meanings through correspondences with conceptualizations of the world. A good example is the lexical item *plain*. The prototypical meaning of *plain* is simple, not decorated or complicated in style, as in *The rooms are quite plain*. However, based on the speaker's experiences, the lexical item *plain* can have other functions. The first is that it means honest and direct, not trying to trick anyone, as in *I will be plain with you*. The second is that it means clear, or easy to see or understand, as in *The instructions were very plain to follow*.

- Lexical items exhibit polysemy. A lexical item has a wide range of discrete senses that are subsumed under one phonological form. In this approach, the different senses of a lexical item are related, treated like members of a large family. They do not share defining features, but rather family resemblances that overlap. The construction of a category for any lexical item should include both its regular and irregular senses. A simple example is the lexical item *run*. The prototypical meaning of *run* is to move using your legs, going faster than when you walk, as in *I had to run to catch the bus*. Peripherally, *run* has two extensions. In the first, it means to go in a particular direction, as in *The road runs along the side of a lake*. In the second, it means to organize or be in charge of something, as in *They run a new restaurant in Leeds*.

- Lexical meaning is embodied, shaped by aspects of an organism's entire body. The category of a lexical item is constructed in terms of networks. The meaning of a lexical item is defined in terms of the actual experiences gained by humans encountering a physical or social world. Lexical items can be described against the realities of life. A clear example is the lexical item *mouth*. Prototypically, it means the opening in the face used for speaking or eating, as in *Don't talk with your mouth full*. Peripherally, it has two extended meanings. One refers to a person considered only as somebody who needs to be provided with food, as in *The world will not be able to support all these starving mouths*. The other refers to the entrance or opening of something, as in *They took a picture near the mouth of the cave*.

An example

A lexical item is associated with a range of distinct senses that form a complex category. An example is the lexical item *strong*. The prototypical zone of the adjective *strong* signifies strength and has different shades of meaning. (a) 'having physical strength', as in *a strong swimmer*. (b) 'having moral strength', as in *a strong woman*, who can endure hardship. (c) 'having a lot of influence', as in *a strong leader*. (d) 'likely to succeed or happen', as in *a strong candidate for the job*. (e) 'not easily upset or frightened', as in *a strong personality*. The peripheral zone of the adjective *strong* signifies other meanings. (a) 'having a lot of taste', as in *strong cheese*. (b) 'containing a lot of a substance', as in *strong coffee*. (c) 'firmly established', as in *a strong marriage*. (d) 'difficult to attack or criticize', as in *a strong argument*. (e) 'having a lot of force, often offending people', as in *The movie has been criticized for strong language*. (= swearing). (f) 'great in number', as in *There was a strong police presence at the demonstration*. The senses are linked to the prototype by a set of semantic principles. Like members of a family, the senses share the general attributes of the category but differ in specific details.

Practice 7.3

The verb *drive*, the adjective *clear* and the noun *table* exhibit multiplicity of meaning. Sketch out the semantic network for each.

1. drive
2. clear
3. table

Critical appraisal

The prototype theory is a response to the classical or check-list theory of linguistic meaning, which dates back to Aristotle. According to this theory, categories should be clearly defined, mutually exclusive and collectively exhaustive. Categories are discrete entities characterized by a set of properties shared by their members. These properties establish the necessary and sufficient conditions for definition and membership. A necessary condition must be met for category membership, while a sufficient condition guarantees it. The conditions are binary, meaning an entity is a category member if it fulfils all conditions, and not if it fails to meet any. Categories have clear boundaries, with all members being of equal status. For example, the lexical item *bird* requires having a beak, wings, feathers and the ability to fly for inclusion. A sparrow meets these conditions, while a penguin does not due to its inability to fly.

However, the classical theory of meaning is associated with some serious problems. First, it is difficult to identify a precise set of conditions that are necessary and sufficient to define a category. There is no single set of conditions that is shared by each member of the category of any lexical item. Secondly, not all categories have clear boundaries. Categories of lexical items display fuzzy boundaries. It is not necessary for a lexical item sense to possess all the attributes for category membership. Thirdly, category members are not equal; categories exhibit typicality. A lexical item gives rise to a typical example, from which the other less typical examples are derived. The asymmetries between category members are called typicality effects. To solve the problems, Cognitive Lexical Semantics adopts the prototype theory of meaning, which emerged from the work of Rosch and her colleagues. According to this theory, humans categorize not by using necessary and sufficient conditions, but by using a prototype, an exemplar or a salient member of a category that assembles its key attributes.

The application of the prototype model to the description of lexical items has offered some practical advantages.

- It embodies the notion of gradation in the characterization of a lexical item. The senses of a lexical item are scalar or gradual, rather than predictable or plus-or-minus. For example, the lexical item *head* has several graded senses. In *She shook her head in disbelief*, it refers to the body part on top of the neck. In *He resigned as head of the department*, it refers to a person in charge of an organization. In *The thought never entered my head*, it refers to the mind or brain. In *She's taller than her sister by a head*, it refers to a measure of distance or height. In *We took our place at the head of the convoy*, it refers to the first person or vehicle in the line. In *The name was placed at the head of the chart*, it refers to the highest or top part of something. Each sense has a different meaning based on the context of the item's usage in a sentence.

- It is all-encompassing, including the converging as well as the diverging senses in the characterization of a lexical item. To clarify the point, let us take an example. The verb *seed* has two meanings that are opposite of each other. Yet, they are included in the same category. In *He seeded the lawn*, it means planting seeds in it, or adding seeds to it. In *He seeded the grapes*, it means extracting or removing the seeds from it. Thus, it permits the study of more phenomena, whereas in pre-cognitive accounts only those exhibiting absolute commonality were deemed amenable to semantic investigation. The prototype model of categorization allows for generality by including uses that have hitherto been treated as exceptions to the rule or left outside the category.

Summary

One of the goals of Cognitive Lexical Semantics is developing the ability to use the lexical resources of language. More specifically, the goal is to expand vocabulary knowledge: learning to know new senses of polysemous lexical items. In Cognitive Lexical Semantics, different senses of a polysemous lexical item can be seen as members of a structured category. The different but related senses of a lexical item are represented by a network in the language user's mind. The network is structured in terms of prototype and periphery. The senses are related by two kinds of categorizing relationships. The first is extension. This is the process of stretching the scope of meaning. The extended sense shares some but not all the properties of the prototype. The second is schematization. This is the process of producing a schema based on what is common to the senses. A schema represents a structure at a higher level of abstraction. It is a pattern that represents an outline of a lexical item. The prototype model of analysis is dynamic. The senses have many different shades of meaning that differ slightly from context to context.

Key takeaways

- Category members share family resemblances that overlap rather than a strict set of defining features.
- Category membership is determined by similarity, rather than identity, to a prominent example.
- Category members differ in status. Salient members are considered better examples than others.
- A fuzzy or unclear boundary separates category members. Attributes do not apply to all members.

Categorization helps to process and organize information more efficiently, thus reducing cognitive load.

Further reading

Original research on the conception of categorization is reported mainly in Rosch (1977, 1978) and Rosch and Mervis (1975). Foundational works within Cognitive Linguistics employing the prototype theory are Kempton (1981), Aitchison (1987), Lakoff (1987), Langacker (1987), Rudzka-Ostyn (1988), Taylor (1989) and Tsohadzidis (1990)

References

Aitchison, Jean. 1987. *Words in the Mind: An Introduction to the Mental Lexicon*. Oxford: Blackwell.

Kempton, Willett. 1981. *The Folk Classification of Ceramics: A Study in Cognitive Prototypes*. New York: Academic Press.

Lakoff, George. 1987. *Women, Fire and Dangerous Things: What Categories Reveal about the Mind*. Chicago, IL: University of Chicago Press.

Langacker, Ronald. 1987. *Foundations of Cognitive Grammar 1: Theoretical Prerequisites*. Stanford, CA: Stanford University Press.

Rosch, Eleanor. 1977. Human Categorisation. Neil Warren. (ed.). *Studies in Cross-Cultural Psychology* 1: 3–49.

Rosch, Eleanor. 1978. Principles of Categorisation. In Eleanor Rosch and Barbara B. Lloyd (eds.), *Cognition and Categorisation*, 27–48. Hillsdale, NJ: Lawrence Erlbaum Associates.

Rosch, Eleanor and Carolyn Mervis. 1975. Family Resemblances: Studies in the Internal Structure of Categories. *Cognitive Psychology* 7 (4): 573–605.

Rudzka-Ostyn, Brygida (ed.). 1988. *Topics in Cognitive Linguistics*. Amsterdam: Benjamins.
Taylor, John. 1989. *Linguistic Categorisation. Prototypes in Linguistic Theory*. Oxford: Clarendon Press.
Tsohadzidis, Savas (ed.). 1990. *Meanings and Prototypes: Studies in Linguistic Categorisation*. London: Routledge.

CHAPTER EIGHT

The frame semantics theory

Preview

This chapter examines the role of configuration in the semantic description of lexical items as groups. The goal is to uncover the unique meaning of each lexical item within a field. **Configuration** refers to the mental act of grouping multiple lexical items into a **frame**, which serves as a knowledge background for describing their meanings. The chapter is structured as follows. The first section serves as the introduction, presenting two contrasting theories of configuration. The **lexical field** theory views configuration as a model that focuses solely on linguistic meaning, while the **frame semantics** theory sees it as a model that considers both linguistic and non-linguistic meanings. The second section delves into the frame semantics theory. The third section outlines its assumptions. The fourth section discusses the implications of the theory on lexical meaning. The fifth section provides a critical appraisal of frame semantics, assessing its feasibility and listing its advantages. The final section summarizes the main points of the chapter.

Introduction

A noteworthy aspect of the lexicon is **lexical relationship**, where linguistic items, whether lexical or grammatical, tend to group together and form sets. While there is consensus that a language's lexicon is more than just a list of independent items but rather a collection of interconnected items, there is a debate surrounding the analysis. The debate revolves around the question: how do the lexical items differ from one another? Different linguists propose two solutions to the question based on their linguistic perspectives. The first is the **lexical field** theory, which suggests that lexical items derive their meaning from their relationships with other items in the same field. This theory, akin to the **dictionary theory**, only considers linguistic aspects. According to this theory, a linguistic item's core meaning is the information provided in its definition. The second solution is the **frame semantics** theory, which analyses the meaning of a linguistic item in the context of the frame it belongs to. A **frame** is a coherent structure of concepts, where each item represents conceptual knowledge derived from human experience. This theory, more like an **encyclopaedia**, takes both linguistic and non-linguistic aspects into consideration. The meaning of a linguistic item encompasses all that is known about its referent.

Frame semantics

In contrast to componential, relational and field semantics, Fillmore specifically introduces frame semantics. It is a theory of linguistic meaning that aims to explain the meaning of lexical items in terms of background frames. This approach to the study of lexical meaning tries to connect linguistic meaning to encyclopaedic knowledge or real-world scenarios provided by frames. According to this theory, the meanings of lexical items can be properly identified, understood or described against the background of a specific body of knowledge known as a *frame*. The central concept in frame semantics is the *frame* itself. A frame is an abstract scenario against which the meanings of related lexical items are understood. It is any system of interconnected concepts where understanding one concept requires understanding the entire system. Using one concept brings all others to mind. A frame is a knowledge structure, represented at the conceptual level, that it encompasses all aspects associated with a culturally embedded event, scene or situation, resulting from human experience.

To grasp the theory, let's briefly examine Fillmore's typical example of the commercial transaction frame. A commercial transaction is an interaction between two parties where something of value is exchanged for payment. In this scenario, background knowledge includes elements like buying, selling, goods and money. These are linked to entities such as the buyer, the seller, the item being sold and the payment method. While these elements are closely connected, they emphasize different aspects of the scene, with each representing a specific facet of the experience. For example, in the sentence *Jane bought a book from Nancy for $10*, the buyer is the subject, the book is the direct object, and Nancy and $10 are propositional phrases. On the other hand, in *Nancy sold a book to Jane for $10*, the seller is the subject. Each element of the commercial transaction provides a frame for defining the meaning of the six verbs buy, sell, pay, charge, spend and cost.

Practice 8.1

The verbs listed below evoke the frame of 'employment'. Yet, each represents a particular facet. What is it?

1. hire
2. employ
3. engage
4. recruit
5. appoint

Assumptions

Frame semantics is an approach to systematically describing meaning in natural language. It is guided by the slogan 'Meanings are relativized to scenes', which implies meanings have an internal structure determined relative to a background frame. In this way, frame semantics incorporates the main theoretical principles of cognitive lexical linguistics: the idea that language is an integral part of cognition, reflecting the interaction of cultural, psychological, communicative and functional considerations. Frame semantics is based on the following basic assumptions.

- The meaning of a lexical item cannot be understood without access to the encyclopaedic knowledge related to the item. This means that meaning in natural language is interconnected with other forms of knowledge. Encyclopaedic knowledge is contained within a frame, which characterizes an abstract scene or situation with its elements. To understand the semantic structure of an element within the frame, one must first understand the properties of the scene or situation and then the properties of the other elements within the frame. For example, to understand the lexical item *sell,* one must have knowledge of a commercial transaction, including a seller, a buyer, goods to be sold and a form of payment.

- A lexical item activates a frame and represents an individual concept within it. A **frame** consists of a set of concepts related in such a way that understanding one requires understanding the entire structure in which it exists. A frame is a coherent structure of related concepts that co-occur in real-world situations. Knowledge of the frame is essential for understanding lexical items referring to the concepts in the frame. In the commercial transaction frame, for instance, the lexical item *sell* describes the situation from the seller's perspective, while the lexical item *buy* describes the situation from the buyer's perspective. Introducing the lexical item *sell* in conversation automatically brings to mind other lexical items in the frame. Individual items derive their meanings from a larger framework of meaning.

- Encyclopaedic knowledge is organized into experiential frames. A frame consists of specific aspects of encyclopaedic knowledge that it evokes, representing things that happen together in reality. These aspects highlight different ways in which the frame can be viewed. Encyclopaedic knowledge serves as the background for describing the aspects. A lexical item evokes a particular frame and profiles an aspect within the frame. Therefore, an evoked frame is the knowledge structure needed to understand a given lexical item, whereas an aspect of a frame symbolizes a specific experience. For example, the commercial transaction frame includes aspects such as selling, buying, money and goods, with two transfers in opposite directions: money from buyer to seller and goods from seller to buyer.

Practice 8.2

The following lexical items evoke the semantic frame of *breaking* or *cutting*. For each item, try to establish the meaning that would distinguish it from its companions in the frame.

1. split
2. chop
3. crack
4. carve
5. divide

Repercussions

The adoption of frame theory has significant repercussions for lexical items, as outlined below.

- Lexical items rely on frames. A frame is a coherent conceptual area that defines the meanings of lexical items. It serves as a context of background knowledge through which lexical items are interpreted. For example, the adjectives *accidental*, *fortuitous* and *casual* derive their meanings from the frame of *chance*. However, each adjective emphasizes a different aspect of the frame. The adjective *accidental* describes something happening unintentionally, as in *The site was found after the accidental discovery of bones in a field*. The adjective *fortuitous* suggests a strong element of chance, as in *His success was due to a fortuitous combination of circumstances.* The adjective *casual* emphasizes a lack of intent or premeditation, as in *It was just a casual comment, I didn't mean any harm.*

- The scope of a lexical item is subdivided into two essential aspects, both of which are indispensable for its meaning. These are the profile and its base, or figure and ground. The **profile** is the specific concept invoked by the lexical item, while the **base** is the frame against which the profile is understood. One implication of the profile-base relation is that the same base can yield different profiles. For instance, the frame of *value* serves as a base for the adjectives *precious, (in)valuable* and *priceless,* each highlighting a distinct aspect. The adjective *precious* describes something as rare and valuable, as in *precious jewels.* The adjective *(in)valuable* emphasizes an extremely useful action, as in *(in)valuable discovery.* The adjective *priceless* signifies something of utmost importance, as in *priceless family photos.*

- Lexical items can evoke multiple frames for interpretation. A lexical item may be associated with more than one frame. The collection of frames that provide the context for fully understanding a lexical item is known as a **matrix**. These frames do not exist independently but interact and influence each other in various ways. For example, when describing the concept of a *father,* the frame of a kinship network must be considered. While this frame captures a significant aspect of the meaning, other frames also come into play. In the frame of physical objects, a *father* is a tangible being with weight and dimensions. In the frame of living things, a *father* is a creature with a lifespan. In the frame of family relations, a *father* holds a crucial role in their children's lives.

An example

The meaning of a lexical item can be defined in terms of the semantic frame it activates. To clarify, let's take an example. The verbs *brush, scrub, sweep, wipe* and *scour* evoke the frame of **cleaning**, but each verb is used in a different context. *Brush* means to clear or make something smooth with a brush. It is used with hair, teeth and clothes, as in *Have you brushed your teeth yet?*, and *You should brush your jacket, it is covered in dust. Scrub* means to clean something by rubbing it hard with a brush and some water or soap. It is used with stains, as in *He is trying to scrub the stain from the carpet. Sweep* means to clean the floor or ground using a brush with a long handle. It is used with floors, as in *When everyone had left, she swept the floor. Wipe* means to clean the surface of something by sliding something, especially a piece of cloth, over it. It is used with porcelain crockery for serving food and drink, as in *She has washed up, and wiped the cups, saucers and plates*. *Scour* means to clean a cooking pan or hard surface by rubbing it with a piece of rough material. It is used with metal containers for cooking food, as in *I scoured the bowls, pots and pans*.

Practice 8.3

The following lexical items activate the semantic frame of 'sending away'. Yet, each has a certain duty to carry out. Use each verb in a sentence to show its meaning.

1. evict
2. expel
3. banish
4. dismiss
5. discharge

Critical appraisal

The theory of frame semantics is a response to the Componential Analysis theory of linguistic meaning, adopted within the generative model. It appeared in Katz and Fodor (1963), and was refined in Katz and Postal (1964) and Katz (1972). According to this theory, the vocabulary of language can be defined in terms of semantic components or primitives. The meaning of lexical items can be analysed as construed from basic semantic features or markers. For instance, the lexical item *bachelor* can be analysed using the components [+MALE, +ADULT, -MARRIED]. The core meaning of a lexical item resides in the information represented by these components. For example, the lexical item *bachelor* means 'unmarried adult male'. Consequently, lexical meaning is defined in terms of intrinsic or non-contextual components, which is the proper sphere of Lexical Semantics. Issues such as how the outside world interacts with linguistic meaning belong to the sphere of pragmatics. Such issues are considered by Componential Analysis theorists to be external to the concerns of linguistics.

While Componential Analysis is useful for describing some aspects of phonology or syntax, and for analysing kinship terms, it is not a representation of how language works. The theory has been criticized in two important ways. The first has to do with the identification of semantic components. No linguist has ever been able to develop a complete list of such components. If semantic components were to exist, they would number in the thousands. Additionally, it proves impossible to agree on the number of components needed for precise definitions of lexical items. The second criticism has to do with the use of metalanguages. The devices used, such as symbols and diagrams, are ad hoc and unsystematic. Attaching a set of components to a lexical item is not semantic analysis in the deepest sense. Translating from the object language into an arbitrary invented language does not advance semantic analysis. Cognitive Lexical Semantics rejects the idea that lexical meaning can be modelled by strict definitions based on semantic decomposition. Lexical items could be understood properly relative to the frames in which they are embedded.

The application of frame semantics to the description of lexical items has offered some practical advantages.

- It is a mechanism for defining the meanings of lexical items. To define an item, it is necessary to understand the entire frame to which it belongs and see which of its aspects it picks out. For example, to define the meanings of the lexical items *land* and *ground*, we need to think of the frame that they evoke. In *I spent three hours on land this afternoon*, the lexical item *land* refers to a sea voyage. In *I spent three hours on the ground this afternoon*, the lexical item *ground* refers to an air journey. Accordingly, lexical items should not be tackled in isolation. Instead, they should be put in juxtaposition and tackled in terms of appropriate frames.

- It is a tool for comparing one lexical item with another. It serves to explicate similarities and differences between or among the member items in a frame, and so is a convenient way of identifying the patterns in which they occur. For example, compare the uses of the prepositions *on* and *in*. The sentence *The children played on the bus* with the preposition *on* describes a scene in which the children were playing while the bus was in operation as a vehicle for transportation. The sentence *The children played in the bus* with the preposition *in* describes a scene in which the children were playing in an abandoned bus in a vacant lot.

Summary

In this chapter, I have argued that lexical items must be interpreted with reference to semantic frames. The meanings of lexical items are understood relative to background frames, which are coherent systems of related concepts representing schematizations of experience. Frames are mental knowledge structures capturing the typical features of a situation. A frame is a situation with many aspects, with each lexical item representing a specific aspect. A frame is a coherent set of related ideas forming the basis for associations with specific lexical items. Therefore, a frame is a device whereby lexical items can be seen as semantically related to one another. The nuances that lexical items display are derived from recognizing the different ways in which they schematize the world. This shows that single lexical items are not meaningful without a larger framework of meaning. Therefore, to understand a lexical item, it is necessary to understand the entire frame, which requires reference to the encyclopaedic meaning provided by a frame. The meanings of lexical items derive from their associations with the background frame, not from associations with other lexical items.

Key takeaways

- Lexical items are not directly related to each other. The meaning of a lexical item depends on the frame to which it belongs, and the particular slot within the frame that it fills.
- Lexical items should be treated as tools that cause readers to activate certain areas of their knowledge network. They are defined by their relationship to the frame's structure.
- The theory recognizes the role of context in assigning a lexical item to a semantic frame. The use of context helps to indicate what speakers do in their natural use of language.
- The theory emphasizes the role of the speaker in construing the world. The use of a lexical item reflects the intention of the speaker and is a response to the communicative needs of discourse.
- The theory is encyclopaedia-based. The meaning of a lexical item includes knowledge of what it means and how it is used, encompassing linguistic and non-linguistic knowledge in the definition.

Further reading

Extensive discussions of the concept of frame are found in Fillmore (1977, 1982), Fillmore and Atkins (1992), Barsalou (1992) and Fontenelle (2003). A similar but not identical concept to the frame is the concept of domain. The concept of domain was introduced to linguistics by Langacker (1987, 1991) and elaborated in Evans and Green (2006), Croft and Cruse (2004) and Hamawand (2023).

References

Barsalou, Lawrence. 1992. Frames, Concepts and Conceptual Fields. In Adrienne Lehrer and Eva Feder Kittay (eds.), *Frames, Fields and Contrasts: New Essays in Semantic and Lexical Organisation*, 21–74. Hillsdale, NJ: Lawrence Erlbaum Associates.

Clausner, Timothy and William Croft. 1999. Domains and Image Schemas. *Cognitive Linguistics* 10 (1): 1–31.

Croft, William and David Alan Cruse. 2004. *Cognitive Linguistics*. Cambridge: Cambridge University Press.

Evans, Vyvyan and Melanie Green. 2006. *Cognitive Linguistics: An Introduction*. Mahwah, NJ: Lawrence Erlbaum Associates.

Fillmore, Charles. 1977. 'Scenes-and-frames'. In Antonio Zampolli (ed.), *Linguistic Structures Processing*, 55–81. Amsterdam: North-Holland Publishing.

Fillmore, Charles. 1982. 'Frame Semantics'. In Linguistic Society of Korea (ed.), *Linguistics in the Morning Calm*, 111–38. Seoul: Hanshin Publishing.

Fillmore, Charles and Beryl Theresa Sue Atkins. 1992. Toward a Frame-based Lexicon: The Semantics of Risk and Its Neighbours. In Adrienne Lehrer and Eva Feder Kittay (eds.), *Frames, Fields and Contrasts: New Essays in Semantic and Lexical Organization*, 75–102. Hillsdale, NJ: Erlbaum. (1994).

Fontenelle, Thierry (ed.). 2003. FrameNet and Frame Semantics. *International Journal of Lexicography* 16 (3): 231–366.

Hamawand, Zeki. 2023. Cognitive Domains. In Thomas Fuyin (ed.), *Handbook of Cognitive Semantics*, 433–61. Leiden: Brill.

Katz, Jerrold Jacob. 1972. *Semantic Theory*. New York: Harper & Row.

Katz, Jerrold Jacob and Jerry Alan Fodor. 1963. The Structure of a Semantic Theory. *Language* 39 (2): 170–210.

Katz, Jerrold Jacob and Paul Martin Postal. 1964. *An Integrated Theory of Linguistic Descriptions*. Cambridge, MA: MIT Press.

Langacker, Ronald. 1987. *Foundations of Cognitive Grammar*. Vol. 1: *Theoretical Prerequisites*. Stanford, CA: Stanford University Press.

Langacker, Ronald. 1991. *Foundations of Cognitive Grammar*. Vol. 2: *Descriptive Application*. Stanford, CA: Stanford University Press.

CHAPTER NINE

The construal theory

Preview

This chapter evaluates the impact of **conceptualization** on explaining pairs of lexical items that act as rivals. The goal is to uncover the differences in meaning between seemingly similar lexical items. **Conceptualization** refers to the mental act of construing a situation in alternate ways. The chapter is structured as follows. The first section serves as the introduction, comparing two theories of explanation. The **reference** theory treats meaning as existing outside the mind, equating it with truth values. On the other hand, the **construal** theory views meaning as existing in the mind, equating it with conceptualization. **Construal** refers to the speaker's mental ability to describe a situation in different ways and express it using various linguistic items. The second section delves into the construal theory. The third section reveals the axioms of the theory. The fourth section underlines the ramifications of the theory regarding lexical meaning. The fifth section is a critical appraisal of the construal theory, assessing its viability and enumerating its advantages. The final section of the chapter gives a summary of the main points of the chapter.

Introduction

An intriguing aspect of the lexicon is **synonymy**, where lexical items tend to have similar meanings. While most theories agree that two or more lexical items can share the same meaning, but they differ on whether these terms can be freely interchanged in context. The crux of the matter lies in the question: In what way are these lexical items distinct? To address this question, linguists from various linguistic backgrounds propose two theories of explanation. The **reference** theory views meaning as objective, with lexical meaning rooted in relationships between lexical items and mind-independent worlds. To distinguish two lexical items as non-synonymous, the choice between them depends on a difference in the objects in the external world that they represent. Conversely, the **construal** theory considers meaning as subjective, with meanings referring more to subjective rather than objective situations, and more discourse rather than described situations. This theory focuses on how language is used by humans to represent, and sometimes even construct, reality. The meaning of a lexical item reflects how a speaker describes a situation.

Construal

The construal theory of meaning is an approach to language that connects the meaning of a lexical item with the idea in the mind of the person who produces it. The meaning of a lexical item is determined by both conceptual content and construal. **Conceptual content** is the inherent property of a situation, conventionally associated with a lexical item. **Construal,** on the other hand, is the way the content is perceived based on communicative needs. A speaker can conceptualize a situation differently and use different lexical items to represent it in discourse. When two lexical items share the same conceptual content, they differ semantically in terms of the alternate ways the speaker construes their common content. Each alternative encodes a distinct meaning, highlighting a different aspect of the content and realized in language differently. For example, the lexical items *convince* and *persuade* describe the same objective situation but with different nuances. *Convince* makes someone believe something is true, whereas *persuade* encourages someone to do something. Construal is a matter of how a situation is conceptualized and linguistically encoded.

Axioms

The construal theory is based on principal axioms, summarized as follows:

- A semantic structure includes both conceptual content and a particular way of construing that content. Two lexical items may invoke the same conceptual content but differ semantically by the construals they represent. The ability of the speaker to construe an objective situation in different ways is fundamental to lexical and grammatical organization. The choice of a lexical item correlates with the particular construal imposed on a situation. For example, the two lexical items *empathy* and *sympathy* involve understanding and caring about someone else's problems, but they are not synonymous. They construe the situation differently, with *empathy* focusing on sharing someone else's feelings, and *sympathy* on being sorry for someone.

- Alternation in a language is not random. Pairs of lexical items are not identical in meaning or equal in use; every two forms contrast in meaning. A difference in form always implies a difference in meaning. Each lexical item has a distinct meaning in the lexicon. Lexical variation is not free, with variants usually displaying subtle differences in meaning or unequal functions in discourse. For example, the two lexical items *authentic* and *genuine* refer to something real but are not synonymous. They construe things differently. *Authentic* suggests something traditional, as in *It is a friendly restaurant offering authentic Greek food*. *Genuine* suggests something as natural, as in *Is the painting a genuine Picasso?*

- Meaning equates roughly with connotation, referring to the idea that a lexical item invokes in addition to its literal meaning. Meaning resides in the association between a lexical item and the indirect or implicit message it suggests. This contrasts with denotation, the explicit or direct meaning of a lexical item. For example, the two lexical items *jealous* and *envious* mean feeling angry or unhappy because one wishes one had an advantage someone else has, but they are not synonymous. They construe the situation differently. *Jealous* implies hostility towards someone who has an advantage, as in *You are just jealous of me because I got better marks*. *Envious* indicates a desire for the same advantage, as in *She has always been envious of her sister's good looks*.

Ramifications

The adoption of the construal theory in describing lexical items has several crucial ramifications.

- Both propositional and non-propositional meanings are significant. Speakers of a language do not consider two lexical forms of the same proposition as synonyms. When a language provides two identical lexical items, speakers find a way to differentiate between them. Each lexical item corresponds to a unique meaning. The difference in meaning is believed to be the result of a specific dimension of construal. For example, the two lexical items *allude* and *refer* share the same proposition, but they differ in construal. *Allude* is used to indirectly state things, as in *The reporter alluded to the president's secret fortune*. *Refer* is used to directly state things, as in *The reporter referred to the $250 million in the president's bank account*.

- Lexical items that occur in the same position do not freely alternate. Their alternation relies heavily on context. Alternatives reflect different conceptualizations, and as a result, are lexically realized differently. Differences in lexical form are not random but indicate differences in meaning. For example, the two lexical items *pick* and *select* have the same proposition, choosing something from many possibilities. However, they differ in construal. The lexical item *pick* means to choose something without much thought, as in *Pick a card from the pack*. The lexical item *select* means to choose after careful consideration, as in *How does the boss select people for promotion?*

- Apparently similar lexical items, whether abstract or concrete, are subject to analysis. They do not stem from the same underlying structure, nor is one derived from the other, as assumed by pre-cognitive approaches. Instead of being seen as lexical variations, they are attributed to distinct semantic values. In cognitive terms, semantics is directly associated with surface form. The form of a lexical item reflects its meaning. For example, although the two lexical items *freedom* and *liberty* mean more or less the same, they are distinguishable in use. *Freedom* means the right to live as one wishes without restraint, as in *He enjoys the freedom of speech*. *Liberty* means release from previous restraint, as in *The released prisoner enjoys his new liberty*.

Dimensions of construal

Construal is a complex phenomenon that reflects our basic cognitive abilities through various dimensions. These dimensions allow us to adjust our focus, transforming one conceptualization into another that is similar in content but different in construal. The semantic value of lexical items is closely tied to the dimensions of construal imposed on their content. When using a specific lexical item, a speaker chooses a dimension from a range of options to structure its conceptual content for communication. This selection determines how attention is focused on different aspects of a situation and how various lexical items are used to describe it. Multiple dimensions of construal contribute to the meaning of a single lexical item, each providing a different perspective on the content.

The dimensions of construal can be categorized under specificity, prominence, perspective and focusing.

Specificity

In Cognitive Grammar, a situation can be perceived at various levels of detail. In language, expressions differ in the level of precision and detail used to characterize a situation. A coarse-grained description, known as schematicity, provides a basic, abstract representation, with minimal detail. On the other hand, a fine-grained description, known as **specificity**, offers a detailed and precise portrayal of a situation. Specificity involves attending to the details of a situation and provides more information compared to schematicity. The choice between these levels of detail influences the meaning of an expression. Thus, the same objective situation can be described at different degrees of detail; each accords the lexical item with a special semantic import.

An example

In Cognitive Grammar, lexical items vary in terms of schematicity or specificity. Each construal plays a crucial role in characterizing the lexical item. Schematicity refers to the degree of generality associated with a lexical item, while specificity refers to the degree of granularity associated with it. This distinction can be seen in a progression from more schematic to more specific lexical choices, such as *thing > creature > person > female > girl*. Each lexical item in this progression is more specific than the one before it, reflecting the ability of speakers to describe situations in abstract or concrete terms. Despite sharing the same conceptual content, lexical items can be semantically different due to the different levels of detail at which they construe that content. This highlights the speaker's ability to describe concepts in multiple ways through lexical choices.

Practice 9.1

The following lexical pairs are exchanged by a large number of people. The lexical pairs however are different in terms of schematicity-specificity dimensions of construal. Show how.

1. work vs. job
2. goal vs. objective
3. illness vs. disease
4. incident vs. accident
5. guarantee vs. warranty

Profiling

As a dimension of construal, **prominence** refers to the quality of eminence given, often in varying degrees, to the substructures of a conception relative to their importance. One type of prominence is profiling. Every linguistic expression consists of a profile imposed on a base. The base is the conceptions activated by the expression, including elements that are both central and peripheral to its meaning. Within its base, every expression singles out a substructure that functions as the focal point of attention. This substructure, the **profile**, is the one that the expression designates. The profile is the portion that functions as a focal point and receives a special degree of prominence. The base constitutes the larger structure, of which the profile constitutes a substructure. The base is essential for understanding the meaning of the profile. The process whereby an aspect of some base is designated is referred to as **profiling**. Profiling involves bringing one part of a concept to the foreground. The particular profile imposed on a base is a consequence of the way the conceptualizer construes a situation, which determines the semantic value of a linguistic expression.

An example

In lexicology, the dimension of profiling can be estimated by examining instances in which profiling designates different aspects of a situation. Linguistically, the lexical item used evokes a distinct frame. For instance, in the following examples the different uses of the lexical item *close* profile different frames as the basis for meaning. This is due to the semantic flexibility that lexical items in general and the lexical item *close* in particular display. In *Our new house is close to the school*, it profiles the frame of space. In *The children are close to each other in age*, it profiles the frame of time. In *The new library is close to completion*, it profiles the frame of state. In *The child is very close to her mother*, it profiles the frame of relationship. In *His feeling for her was close to hatred*, it profiles the frame of similarity. In *She's always been very close with her money*, it profiles the frame of meanness. In *He was so close about his past*, it profiles the frame of secrecy. In *Can I open the window? It's very close in here*, it profiles air conditions, in which it is uncomfortably warm. Each variant profiles the conceptualized scene differently.

Practice 9.2

Identify the cognitive frame that the lexical item *far* profiles in each of the following expressions.

1. She does not live far from here.
2. They worked far into the night.
3. You are getting far too cheeky!
4. I read as far as the third chapter.
5. The story sounds very far-fetched.
6. He is the most far-sighted politician.

7. The law has far-reaching benefits for workers.
8. She was so far gone that she could hardly walk.
9. The advantages far outweigh the disadvantages.
10. He's a very talented writer. I'm sure she'll go far.

Vantage point

As a dimension, perspective refers to the particular way of viewing a situation, which can shift according to one's intention. Describing a situation often involves shifting attention or emphasis from one part to another, depending on the needs of the discourse. One type of perspective is the **vantage point**, which refers to the position from which the same objective situation is observed and described, resulting in different perspectives and different structures. The vantage point is the physical location of the participants in the speech situation: either the speaker or the hearer. It can also refer to time and the attitudinal stances of the speaker. The importance of the vantage point is twofold. Conceptually, the vantage point serves as a window through which the speech-act participants can observe the described scene, and helps to specify which participant is involved in the described scene. Lexically, the vantage point yields a distinction between expressions where the scene is construed from an external vantage point, i.e. from outside of a thing, and expressions where the scene is construed from an internal vantage point, i.e. from inside a thing.

An example

In lexicology, the dimension of the vantage point is crucial in examining instances in which the same objective scene is viewed. A vantage point is a location from which a situation is apprehended. The motion verbs in *Sara came in* and *Sara went in* reflect a shift in perspective. They inherently adopt the speaker's viewpoint and designate motion towards or away from him or her, respectively. The first involves the vantage point of the person who is inside the place, and the motion is directed towards the person. Therefore, the person's viewpoint is described by using the verb *come*. The second involves the vantage point of the person who is outside the place, and the motion is directed away from the person. Therefore, the person's viewpoint is described by using the verb *go*. Thus, the two lexical items presuppose different speaker locations: inside and outside the place, respectively. This shows that some expressions have a built-in viewpoint on a situation, and invoke a vantage point as part of their meaning. The linguistic description of a scene depends on the vantage point we assume.

Practice 9.3

The following lexical items describe the same situation but do so from different vantage points. Account for what each is all about.

1. coast vs. shore
2. borrow vs. lend
3. floor vs. ground
4. external vs. exterior
5. emigrate vs. immigrate

Subjectivity-objectivity

Another type of perspective concerns the subjectivity-objectivity distinction. Subjectivity and objectivity represent different ways of viewing reality: one is based on personal experiences, while the other is rooted in facts. When it comes to **subjectivity,** the speaker is emotionally involved in the situation being described. The speaker includes himself or herself as part of the scene he or she describes, creating a close relationship between the speaker and the content of the situation. Subjectivity focuses on individual experiences and personal aspects of life, emphasizing internal reality. On the other hand, **objectivity** involves the speaker maintaining a sense of distance from the situation being described. The speaker excludes himself or herself from the scene he or she describes, establishing a more detached relationship between the speaker and the content of the situation. Objectivity focuses on general situations that are shared by or affect most people, not just the speaker. It emphasizes external reality.

An example

In the field of lexicology, the dimensions of subjectivity and objectivity are essential when analysing how reality is perceived. A subjectively construed expression is one where the speaker relates the situation described exclusively to the self. In contrast, an objectively construed expression is one where the speaker relates the situation described exclusively to the public. For example, the lexical items *surmise* and *deduce* both involve making educated guesses or inferences, but there is a subtle difference between the two. *Surmise* entails making an inference based on incomplete or uncertain information, relying on personal opinions, as in *From the way he was dressed, she surmised that he was a businessman*. *Deduce*, on the other hand, involves drawing a logical conclusion based on established facts or evidence, relying on impartial judgement and unbiased observations, as in

Based on his fingerprints, the detective deduced that the suspect was at the scene of the crime. Confusing these terms can lead to misunderstandings and inaccuracies.

Practice 9.4

Specify the subjective-objective dimensions of construal that are imposed on the conceptual content of the following pairs of lexical items.

1. assure vs. ensure
2. accuse vs. charge
3. adverse vs. averse
4. delusion vs. illusion
5. certitude vs. certainty

Scope

As a dimension of construal, **focusing** refers to the ability of the speaker to pay attention to one particular part of an expression rather than another. The specific part that is singled out for attention, based on the requirements of communication, is called the **focus**. Linguistically, the expression is encoded in a particular form. One type of focusing is **scope**, which is defined as the array of content a predication specifically evokes for its characterization. The scope of an expression includes the extent of conceptual content that it evokes as the basis for its meaning. Subsumed under scope are the immediate scope and maximal scope. The **immediate scope** contains the profile and represents the general locus of attention. It is the part of an expression that is directly under consideration. The immediate scope is the one with the highest degree of prominence and relevance. The **maximal scope** is the full range of content that an expression evokes. The maximal scope is vague and non-delimited in reference. It includes everything a speaker is aware of at a given moment to assess the meaning of an expression.

An example

The construal of scope can be applied to different areas of language with equal effect. In addition to syntactic patterns, the construal of scope can be applied to lexical patterns. Scope refers to the limits of what humans can and need to mentally focus on at one time. A lexical item has both a maximal and immediate scope. A maximal scope is a larger domain of knowledge selected by the item. It is the full extent of its coverage. An immediate scope is a smaller and more relevant part of the item. It is the portion directly relevant to the meaning of the item. For instance, the lexical items *terse* and *verbose* are both adjectives used to describe the mode of writing. However, they differ in terms of scope, and are consequently used in different contexts. The lexical item *terse* refers to a narrow scope. Terse language means using only the essential words to convey the message, as in *He issued a statement that is terse and concise.* In contrast, the lexical item *verbose* refers to a broad scope. Verbose language means using more words than necessary to convey a message, as in *She gave a reply that is verbose and complex.*

Practice 9.5

The following lexical items have a similar core meaning, but differ as to the size of their scope. Explain.

1. review vs. revise
2. gather vs. collect
3. extend vs. expand
4. specimen vs. sample
5. dilemma vs. quandary

Foreground-background distinction

Another type of focusing relates to the foreground-background distinction. The act of perception usually involves the foregrounding of some portion of the perceptual field called the **figure** and the backgrounding of the rest called the **ground**. Attention is focused on the figure, which is thereby more fully present to consciousness than the ground. It is that part which is more salient or stands out against the rest of the scene. In language, the meanings of all linguistic items are described against a base of foreground or background knowledge. **Foregrounding**, sometimes called **highlighting**, is the act of giving the most importance to a particular part of an expression. **Backgrounding** is the act of paying less attention and therefore less importance to a part of an expression. **Foregrounding** is used for specific communicative purposes. Like perceivers who can divide any given spatial scene into a figure and a ground, speakers can impose the foreground-background status on any given element within an expression, by placing a portion of the construction in the foreground or background of attention. The distinction between foreground and background is analogous to the distinction between figure and ground in visual perception.

An example

The foreground-background distinction can be applied to lexicology. To communicate effectively, we must decide which elements of our intended message to foreground, and which can remain in the background. For instance, consider the difference between the lexical items *gist* and *crux*. When the speaker wants to foreground the general idea of something, he or she uses the noun *gist*, as in *She missed the gist of the argument*. In this conceptualization, the general meaning of the argument is foregrounded. *Gist* refers to the general aspect of something under consideration. When the speaker wants to foreground the main point of something or the key point about something, he or she uses the noun *crux*, as in *Now we come to the crux of the matter*. In this conceptualization, the central idea of the argument is foregrounded. *Crux* refers to the central aspect of something under consideration. As is clear, the two lexical items are often used interchangeably, but they have distinct meanings due to the construal imposed on the content.

Practice 9.6

The following pairs of lexical items indicate the same situation but highlight different parts in focus. What are they?

1. imply vs. infer
2. whole vs. entire
3. assume vs. presume
4. replace vs. substitute
5. bother vs. disturb

Critical appraisal

The theory of construal is a response to the truth-conditional or objectivist theory of linguistic meaning, developed within the generative model. This theory posits that a statement is true if it corresponds to a state of affairs in the world. It assumes an objective external reality against which lexical descriptions in language can be evaluated as true or false. This is achieved by first translating natural language sentences into a logical metalanguage, and then establishing how the logical form derived corresponds to a specific model of reality. To determine the truth of a statement, the state of affairs in the world must align for it to be true. For example, to understand the meaning of a sentence like *It is cloudy*, one must know what conditions in the world would make the sentence true. A glance at the sky is sufficient to determine the truth of the statement. Linguistic meaning is then defined in terms of the conditions necessary for a sentence to be true. If two sentences express the same state of affairs in the world, they are considered synonymous or equivalent.

The generative approach is not relevant to the current analysis for several reasons. It can only explain the meaning of a subset of utterance types and does not account for expressions that do not convey propositions such as questions, commands and greetings. It contrasts with the experientialist view adopted within Cognitive Lexical Semantics, which defines meaning in terms of human construal of reality. Meaning is seen as a relationship between language and the world, mediated by the human mind. Unlike truth-conditional semantics, which excludes cognitive organization from the linguistic system, Cognitive Lexical Semantics views meaning as the connection between lexical items and the world. It emphasizes the importance of extra-linguistic information in defining a lexical item, and considers the role of the speaker in construing a situation. There is a correlation between conceptual structure and human interaction with the sensory experience. Conceptual structure is embodied, meaning that the organization of concepts arises from bodily experience. The meanings associated with lexical items are seen as reflections of thoughts, representing the various ways a speaker construes a given situation.

The application of the construal model to the description of lexical items has offered some practical benefits.

- It enables speakers to conceptualize a situation in different ways, resulting in different lexical manifestations. For example, *evade* and *avoid* both mean 'prevent something from happening', but they have distinct differences in meaning. To *evade* is to cleverly escape from or avoid capture. It implies a more cunning or agile escape, as in *He evaded capture*. To *avoid* is to deliberately and consciously stay away from a dangerous or undesirable experience. It means to steer clear a person, situation or thing, as in *Jim avoids the company of gamblers*. Of the two lexical items, *evade* usually has a negative connotation.

- It solicits semantic as well as pragmatic factors in determining the selection of a lexical item. For example, the lexical items *across* and *through* refer to the movement from one side of something to the other. Still, there is a difference in meaning. In *She walked across the tunnel*, the lexical item *across* implies movement across the top of the tunnel, e.g. if it is underground and the road goes over it. In *She walked through the tunnel*, the lexical item *through* suggests entering and exiting a space. Pragmatically, *across* involves movement in a two-dimensional open space, whereas *through* involves movement in a three-dimensional enclosed space.

Summary

In this chapter, I have argued that an important aspect of meaning is the speaker's ability to construe a situation in multiple ways. The ability is captured in the concept of construal, where the speaker conceives the conceptual content in alternative ways and selects appropriate language structures to express it. Different lexical items may invoke the same conceptual content, but differ semantically due to the construals imposed on their content. Each construal represents a distinct meaning. Alternative conceptual choices lead to different lexical manifestations. Construal is a mental operation that allows the speaker to choose a particular image from various alternatives to structure a situation's content. Language, whether lexical or grammatical, encodes different conceptualizations of experience. Cognitive Lexical Semantics embraces a subjectivist view of meaning, suggesting that a lexical item's meaning involves not only inherent properties but also the way the conceptualizer chooses to construe its conceptual content.

Key takeaways

- Lexical items are markers of construal, representing different ways of conceiving and expressing a situation. The form of a lexical item reflects a specific kind of construal imposed on its structure.

- Lexical items embody various dimensions of construal that speakers use to describe situations. Construal allows the speaker to describe the same content in different ways.

- Lexical alternatives are not equal. They are subtly different. Each alternative has a specific function. The construal theory challenges the idea of synonymy in language.

- Our understanding of the world is not solely based on objective reality but heavily influenced by subjective interpretations. Speakers may have different reactions to the same situation.

- Construals are influenced by motivational factors such as goals, desires and needs. Our motivations shape how we perceive the environment and interact with the world.

Further reading

The notion of construal in Cognitive Grammar is dealt with in Langacker (1993, 2015, 2019), Hamawand (2021), Taylor and MacLaury (1995), Talmy (2006), Verhagen (2007), Achard (2008), Pleyer (2017) and Pütz and Dirven (1996).

References

Achard, Michel. 2008. Teaching Construal: Cognitive Pedagogical Grammar. In Peter Robinson and Nick Ellis (eds.), *Handbook of Cognitive Linguistics and Second Language Acquisition*, 442–65. New York: Routledge.

Hamawand, Zeki. 2021. Construal. In Xu Wen and John Taylor (eds.), *The Routledge Handbook of Cognitive Linguistics*, 242–54. London: Routledge. Amsterdam: Benjamins.

Langacker, Ronald. 1993. Universals of Construal. *Berkeley Linguistics Society* 19: 447–63.

Langacker, Ronald. 2015. Construal. In Ewa Dabrowska and Dagmar Divjak (eds.), *Handbook of Cognitive Linguistics*, 120–42. Berlin: De Gruyter Mouton.

Langacker, Ronald. 2019. Construal. In Ewa Dąbrowska and Dagmar Divjak (eds.), *Cognitive Linguistics: Foundations of Language*, 140–64. Berlin: Gruyter.

Pleyer, Michael. 2017. Protolanguage and Mechanisms of Meaning Construal in Interaction. *Language Sciences* 63 (1): 69–90.

Pütz, Martin and René Dirven (eds.). 1996. *The Construal of Space in Language and Thought*. Berlin: Gruyter.

Talmy, Leonard. 2006. Grammatical Construal: The Relation of Grammar to Cognition. In Dirk Geeraerts (ed.), *Cognitive Linguistics: Basic Readings*, 69–108. Berlin: Mouton de Gruyter.

Taylor, John and Robert Maclaury (eds.). 1995. *Language and the Cognitive Construal of the World*. Berlin: Gruyter.

Verhagen, Arie. 2007. Construal and Perspectivisation. In Dirk Geeraerts and Hubert Cuyckens (eds.), *The Oxford Handbook of Cognitive Linguistics*, 48–81. Oxford: Oxford University Press.

B

Conceptual mappings

Conceptual mappings are mental operations that establish correspondence between two conceptual domains, where an element in the first domain corresponds to its counterpart in the second. It is an operation that links the properties of one domain with its counterpart in another domain. The mapping occurs between two conceptual domains, where an element from the source domain is mapped onto the target domain. Mapping occurs through the use of conceptual structures such as metaphor, metonymy and blending. **Metaphor** is the process in which a lexical item that designates one thing is used to designate another, making an implicit comparison, as in *a sea of troubles*. **Metonymy** is the process in which one lexical item is substituted for another closely associated with it, as in using *crown* to refer to a *monarch*. **Blending** is the process in which two lexical items are combined to form a new one, as in *Brexit* (Britain + exit). These are considered **conceptual structures**: representation of concepts in the human mind. They help make language more impactful. Under the traditional view, conceptual structures are seen as mere figures of speech used as linguistic embellishments or decorations to ordinary language. Under the cognitive view, they are linguistic manifestations of the workings of the human mind.

Characteristics

- Conceptual mappings involve the ability to think in abstract terms and identify connections between seemingly unrelated concepts. By relating one concept to another, through metaphor or metonymy, individuals can create new ideas and perspectives.

- Conceptual mappings often occur across different domains, such as mapping spatial concepts to temporal concepts or mapping physical experiences to abstract concepts. These cross-domain connections help individuals make sense of unfamiliar ideas.

- Conceptual mappings require cognitive flexibility to consider multiple perspectives and interpretations. This flexibility allows individuals to navigate different conceptual frameworks, adapt their thinking to different contexts, and facilitate the transfer of knowledge.

- Conceptual mappings involve creative thinking processes, allowing for the exploration of different ideas and associations between concepts. This can lead to the generation of innovative ideas, and foster a comprehensive understanding of a subject.

- Conceptual mappings are often used in problem-solving tasks by applying knowledge from one domain to address challenges in another domain. This process allows individuals to leverage existing knowledge and skills to effectively solve new problems.

- Conceptual mappings provide a powerful framework for organizing, analyzing, and communicating complex information. By mapping, individuals can effectively convey and comprehend ideas, thus facilitating effective communication.

CHAPTER TEN

The conceptual metaphor theory

Preview

This chapter explores the role of conceptual metaphors in constructing meaning. **Conceptual metaphor** is a form of figurative language that describes an object or action in a way that isn't literally true, but helps to explain it easily. A metaphor refers to a lexical item that means something different from its literal definition. The aim is to show that metaphors can be a tremendous help when one wants to make a complex thought easier to understand. The chapter is organized as follows. The first section is the introduction, discussing the difference between the two techniques of writing: figurative and non-figurative language. The second section presents the theory of metaphor. The third section discloses the principles of the theory. The fourth section highlights the implications of the theory on lexical meaning. The fifth section mentions the benefits of the theory of metaphor to lexical meaning. The last section summarizes the main ideas of the chapter.

Introduction

There are two effective techniques of speaking and writing: non-figurative and figurative language. **Non-figurative** language, also known as literal language, uses the exact meaning of lexical items without imagination or exaggeration. It maintains a consistent meaning regardless of the context and delivers information straightforwardly and factually. Non-figurative language is required for clear and succinct communication. **Figurative** language, also known as non-literal language, goes beyond the dictionary meaning of lexical items. It uses lexical items in a way that deviates from their conventionally accepted meanings to convey a more complicated meaning or heightened effect. Figurative language adds depth and originality to writing. In figurative language, lexical items are employed in an innovative way to conjure up in the reader's or listener's mind a vivid picture. Figurative language can take multiple forms such as simile, metaphor or metonymy. For example, in *Her lips are red* the sentence uses no figurative language. Every lexical item in the sentence means exactly what it says. In *Her lips are rosy*, the sentence uses a metaphor. The speaker compares the red beauty of a rose with that of the woman's lips.

Metaphor

Metaphor is a form of conceptual structure that involves mapping between two things from distinct areas of knowledge, where one is compared with the other. Metaphor makes a comparison by stating that one thing is something else. In the mapping, aspects of a more familiar area of knowledge, called the **source**, are placed in comparison with aspects of a less familiar area of knowledge called the **target**. Typically, the source is concrete, whereas the target is abstract. The purpose of the comparison is to portray the target in a way that makes it more accessible to human understanding. In the sphere of lexicology, metaphor is an extension in the use of a lexical item beyond its primary sense to describe a referent that bears similarity to the primary referent of the lexical item. In metaphor, a lexical item is applied to a thing to which it is literally not applicable. That is, it conveys meaning beyond the literal meaning of the lexical item. The use of metaphor enables the language user to visualize and describe two similar things. It helps the reader imagine and even feel the thing. It gives the reader a clearer idea of what the thing is like. It creates an atmosphere that helps to understand things better.

Principles

- Metaphor is a cognitive mechanism, not just a rhetorical device in language. It is considered an integral part of human cognition. It helps us understand abstract or complex ideas by mapping them onto concrete or familiar concepts. It is a process that helps to conceptualize a particular concept in different ways. For example, the concept of intimacy can be thought of sometimes in terms of heat, as in *Alan is such a cold person*, and sometimes in terms of distance as in *Alan is quite unapproachable*. As the examples show, metaphor serves to highlight individual aspects of the target concept, which are realized differently in language. Metaphor is often used to add colour or emphasis to the point one is trying to get across.

- Metaphor involves mapping the characteristics of the source domain onto the target domain. The metaphor works by comparing two things by transferring knowledge from the source to the target, by saying that one thing is like the other. In the following examples, the first lexical item is not used literally but metaphorically, as in *book a flight* (buy a ticket in advance), *steal the headlines* (get more attention), and *table a motion* (suggest something for discussion). In *I see the point* (understand the point), the source domain is the physical act of seeing, while the target domain is the mental act of understanding. The examples demonstrate how metaphor helps to increase vocabulary by adding new meanings to existing lexical items.

- Metaphor is embodied. The source domain of metaphors is often grounded in our bodily experiences and sensory perceptions. Through metaphoric mappings, physical aspects of the human body influence the way we understand abstract concepts. In some examples, the metaphor can be based on similarity in shape as in *arm of chair, hand of clock, leg of table, eye of needle* and *mouth of river*. In others, it can be based on spatial relationships as in *face of building, brow of hill, foot of bed* and *head of table*. The examples reflect how human aspects are mapped onto non-human objects. These metaphors have been conventionalized because their meanings are so entrenched in the language community through repeated uses that they become automatic.

An example

As previously mentioned, metaphor is a cognitive mechanism in which a lexical item means something different from its literal definition. In metaphor, the literal interpretation would often be pretty silly. A good example is *My heart is a bottomless ocean of love*. In this metaphor, the abstract domain of love is understood in terms of the concrete domain of the ocean. The metaphor compares the heart with the ocean which it resembles in some respect. The speaker is comparing the depth of his love to the depth of an ocean. The heart is the target domain; the conceptual domain that we try to understand through the use of the source domain. The ocean is the source domain; the conceptual domain from which we draw the metaphorical expression. The shared characteristic between the two domains is depth. The heart is as deep as the ocean. The heart is filled with love just like the ocean filled with water. As can be seen, the structure of the source domain is mapped onto the target domain, and so helps to shape its meaning. The use of metaphor brings a powerful image to mind. It is an effective way to convey an idea.

Patterns

As previously mentioned, metaphor is more than just a figure of speech; it is a cognitive process that implicitly compares two unrelated things, by equating one with another. This comparison makes description easier to visualize and understand, assuming a perceived similarity between a source and a target domain or between a concrete and an abstract concept. Through this comparison, we can bring one idea into the conceptual space of another. The tendency to compare two dissimilar things is a very human activity. In language, metaphors are realized by the use of lexical items, which in some contexts, are to be interpreted as metaphors, not literally. The most common process by which a lexical item acquires an additional meaning is through metaphoric extension. The metaphoric meaning of a lexical item is derived from its literal meaning and contains the same characteristics. Metaphors are pervasive in everyday life and can be found in different parts of speech. Below is a description of each pattern.

Noun metaphors

A noun metaphor is used to describe somebody or something else, in a way that differs from its basic use. The purpose is to show that the two things have similar qualities, making the description more powerful. In the following sentences, the italicized nouns are used metaphorically, not literally, to convey ideas more effectively.

She is *a peach*.	She is compared to a peach for being wonderful, pleasing and helpful.
She is *a sheep*.	She is compared to a sheep for being weak, helpless and easily led.
My father is *a rock*.	The father is compared to a rock for being very strong and reliable.
Your room is *a cowshed*.	The room is compared to a cowshed for being filthy and cluttered.
He is *a thorn* in my side.	He is compared to a thorn for causing trouble, distress and irritation.
Life is *a highway*.	Life is compared to a road for having twists, turns, ups, and downs.
He was *a cheetah* in the race.	The runner's speed is compared to a Cheetah's speed for being very fast.

That lawyer is *a shark*.	The lawyer is compared to a shark for being aggressive, unethical and ruthless.
My teacher is *a monster*.	The teacher is compared to a monster for being extremely wicked and cruel.
John is *a pig*.	John is compared to a pig for being greedy, dirty and unpleasant.

Practice 10.1

Explain the meaning of the metaphor that each of the following underlined nouns manifests.

1. Life is a maze.
2. Love is a journey.
3. Her home is a prison.
4. My home is my castle.
5. The area is an anthill.

Verb metaphors

A verb metaphor is used as an alternative description of an action to add new meaning to the replaced verb. It is the case in which a verb is applied to an object to which it is not literally applicable. The purpose is to add depth to the descriptions of the actions. In the following sentences, the italicized verbs are not used literally but rather metaphorically.

Her heart *sank* on hearing the news.	The sinking of the heart is like going down to the bottom. It means she becomes sad about the news.
She *flew* past me on her bicycle.	The speed of her riding is like the speed of a plane, being very high.
Nutritious food helps *fight* disease.	Recovering from an illness is like fighting a war.
The cold air *pierced* his skin.	Cutting through a person's skin is like cutting something with a sharp object.
Her heart *melts* when she sees him.	The melting of the heart is like the melting of a substance. It means she is filled with compassion or sympathy.

She *constructed* a strong argument.	Constructing an argument is like building a house.
She *resisted* the temptation.	Resisting a temptation is like refusing to accept something and trying to prevent it.
She *breezed* through the task.	Breezing through the task is like the blowing of a current of air. It means she finished it effortlessly.
The book *kindled* my interest.	Kindling an interest is like causing a fire to start with wood.
His head was *spinning* with ideas.	The head spinning with ideas is like something that rotates rapidly. It means that he has a great many ideas in rapid succession.

Practice 10.2

Explain the meaning of the metaphor that each of the following underlined verbs reflects.

1. She hurt my feelings.
2. I am swimming in emails.
3. Her temper flared at the criticism.
4. He dug up information on the market.
5. He broke into their conversation.

Adjective metaphors

An adjective metaphor is a lexical item that describes a noun by denoting a quality that is substituted with another to establish a similarity between them. The purpose is to make the metaphor more explicit, highlighting its presence and emphasizing its meaning. In the following sentences, the italicized adjectives are not used literally but rather metaphorically.

His heart was *broken*.	A broken heart suffers intense emotional pain from experiencing great loss or deep longing.
He is *a shady* character.	A shady character describes someone as being dishonest or unlawful

He gave me *a cold* look.	A cold look is a facial expression that looks very unpleasant or unfriendly.
That's *a dense* paragraph.	A dense paragraph is writing that is too detailed, making it difficult to absorb.
Your excuses smell *fishy*.	A fishy excuse is one that does not seem to be truthful or honest.
I was very *attached to* her.	Being attached to someone means you like that person very much.
His claims are *indefensible*.	An indefensible claim is one that cannot be justified because it is completely wrong.
It was a very *stormy* relationship.	A stormy relationship is one with many disagreements and quarrels.
She has such *a bubbly* personality.	A bubbly personality is someone who bubbles with enthusiasm, energy, and joy.
He had *a heated* argument with her.	A heated argument is one that is full of angry and excited feelings.

Practice 10.3

Show how the underlined adjective metaphor in each of the following sentences enhances the meaning.

1. She is love-starved.
2. He has a heart of gold.
3. He is a straight shooter.
4. She was deeply moved.
5. It is a budding relationship.

Advantages

The adoption of metaphoric language in describing new experiences has provided some practical advantages.

- Metaphors are a powerful means of expression because they can enhance understanding by clarifying complex ideas and connecting them to familiar concepts. They improve the expression of complicated messages by comparing abstract subject matters to familiar items or issues. Metaphors allow for expressing things that are difficult to convey through literal language. For example, in *Frank is a couch potato*, the abstract concept of idleness is illustrated by comparing it to a tangible object like a potato.

- Metaphors make writing vivid and memorable. They add spice to writing and make words sing, making language more colourful, interesting and entertaining. They enable writers to create stronger descriptions with a lasting impact. Metaphors help convey emotions and ideas that may be challenging to express literally. For example, in *I was boiling with anger* the speaker's emotion is described in a richer, more vivid way than simply stating anger.

- Metaphors facilitate communication by enhancing the persuasive power of a message. They can stimulate interest in a topic, and make people think about it more deeply. Metaphors allow writers to convey a lot of information concisely. For example, in *I am drowning in work*, the speaker isn't literally drowning but conveying being overwhelmed with work.

Summary

This chapter has outlined the typical characteristics of the cognitive operation of metaphor. A metaphor is a comparison between two unrelated things without explicitly stating the comparison. In Cognitive Linguistics, metaphors are not just a stylistic feature but a cognitive process that is constantly used. Cross-domain mappings occur between the things compared, where the qualities of one thing are figuratively applied to another. Metaphor transfers knowledge from a familiar subject (source domain) to an unfamiliar one (target domain), reflecting abstract concepts through concrete ones. As an important cognitive tool, metaphor reflects the conceptualization of abstract concepts via concrete ones. Accordingly, metaphor is seen as an important aspect of creativity in language.

Key takeaways

- Metaphor isn't merely additive, i.e. just meant to embellish language or spice it up. Metaphor shapes our understanding of relationships between things in the world.

- Metaphor directly compares two seemingly different things with a common characteristic. Unlike simile, metaphor does not use *like* or *as* in the comparison.

- Metaphor involves mapping between two conceptual domains: source and target. The target is the thing being described. The source is the thing used to describe it.

- Metaphor allows for conveying vivid imagery beyond literal meanings, making it easier to understand.

- Metaphor is pervasive. It is not limited to poetic language or literary texts. It is found in different parts of speech, helping individuals make sense of the environment.

Further reading

The cognitive theory of metaphor is elaborated in Lakoff and Johnson (1980), Paprottée and Dirven (1985), Ricoeur (1987), Lakoff (1987), Lakoff and Turner (1989), Gibbs and Steen (1999), Kövecses (2002), Gibbs (1994, 2015) and Graddy (2007).

References

Gibbs, Raymond. 1994. *The Poetics of Mind*. Cambridge: Cambridge University Press.
Gibbs, Raymond. 2015. Metaphor. In Ewa Dabrowska and Dagmar Divjak (eds.), *Handbook of Cognitive Linguistics*, 167–89. Berlin: De Gruyter Mouton.
Gibbs, Raymond Wayne and Gerard Johannes Steen. 1999. *Metaphor in Cognitive Linguistics*. Amsterdam: John Benjamins.
Graddy, Joseph. 2007. Metaphor. In Dirk Geeraerts and Hubert Cuyckens (eds.), *The Oxford Handbook of Cognitive Linguistics*, 188–213. Oxford: Oxford University Press.
Kövecses, Zoltán. 2002. *Metaphor: A Practical Introduction*. Oxford: Oxford University Press.
Lakoff, George. 1987. *Women, Fire and Dangerous Things: What Categories Reveal about the Mind*. Chicago, IL: University of Chicago Press.
Lakoff, George and Mark Johnson. 1980. *Metaphors We Live By*. Chicago, IL: University of Chicago Press.
Lakoff, George and Mark Turner. 1989. *More than Cool Reason: A Field Guide to Poetic Metaphor*. Chicago, IL: University of Chicago Press.
Paprottée, Wolf and René Dirven (eds.). 1985. *The Ubiquity of Metaphor: Metaphor In Language and Thought*. Amsterdam: Benjamins.
Ricoeur, Paul. 1987. *The Rule of Metaphor: The Rule of Metaphor: The Creation of Meaning in Language*. London: Routledge.

CHAPTER ELEVEN

The conceptual metonymy theory

Preview

This chapter explores the role of conceptual metonymy in meaning construction. **Conceptual metonymy** is a form of figurative language, in which one conceptual entity provides mental access to another with which it has a close association. In other words, metonymy involves a change of name within the same knowledge domain. The chapter aims to show how crucial metonymy is in enhancing understanding and fostering efficient communication. The chapter is organized as follows. The first section is the introduction, discussing the difference between the two techniques of writing: conventional and unconventional. The second section presents the theory of metonymy. The third section discloses the principles of the theory. The fourth section highlights the effects of the theory on lexical meaning. The fifth section enumerates the advantages of the theory of metonymy for lexical meaning. The chapter's key points are outlined in the last section.

Introduction

To understand the world, language users rely on both conventional and unconventional expressions. Both types of expressions can improve writing and communication skills. **Conventional expressions** have literal meanings and follow established norms. The literal meaning of an expression is basic, original or usual. **Unconventional** expressions, on the other hand, have non-literal meaning and do not adhere to convention. They are out of the ordinary and go beyond the dictionary meaning. This is demonstrated by figurative language in which a lexical item used does not have a literal meaning. In this case, the language user has to extend the language system in a motivated, but unpredictable way. This is often seen in figurative language, where lexical items are used in non-literal ways. In *The British Police will get involved in the issue*, for example, the idea is expressed using conventional language. Every lexical item has its direct meaning. In *The Scotland Yard will get involved in the issue* the idea is expressed using unconventional language, through the use of metonymy. A place name *The Scotland Yard* is used to represent the *British police*.

Metonymy

Metonymy is a conceptual structure that involves mapping between two things within the same area of knowledge. In this structure, the name of one thing is substituted for the name of another with which it is associated in some way. In the mapping, the thing called the **target** is not called by its name, but by the name of the thing called the **source**, with which it is closely associated. Usually, the source is more prominent than the target. The purpose of this substitution is to help human understanding by portraying the target in a more understandable way. Metonymy is based on contiguity or association, where two things are closely related and can be used interchangeably. This association is central to creativity, as it allows ordinary lexical items to carry deeper meanings. By using a lexical item to represent another, deeper significance can be conveyed in what may seem like a simple item. Metonymy allows for brevity by replacing complex ideas by shorter, simpler stand-ins. This can make communication more efficient and effective.

Principles

- Reference point: Metonymy is a conceptual operation where one entity, the source, is used to refer to another entity, the target, with which it is associated. The association is in the same domain. For example, in *The land is owned by the Crown*, the lexical item *crown* indirectly refers to the *monarch*. This relationship is like a part-whole connection, where the part *crown* serves as the reference point for accessing the whole concept of the *monarch*. In *The Times hasn't arrived yet*, the lexical item *Times* is used to represent the reporter associated with the newspaper. This relationship is a whole-part connection, where the whole *Times* serves as the reference point for accessing the part of the *reporter*. The examples illustrate how metonymy helps people conceptualize the world.

- Cognitive basis: Metonymy is rooted in cognitive processes and how humans think and categorize information. It involves one conceptual entity, the source, providing access to another entity, the target, within the same domain. Metonymy reflects how we understand the world and connect related concepts. It shows how specific lexical items can represent associated concepts. This phenomenon allows one concept to lead to another within the same domain. For instance, in *Can you give me a hand?* the lexical item *hand* leads to the concept of *help*. In *She speaks in her mother tongue*, the lexical item *tongue* leads to the concept of *language*.

- Contextual dependence: The meaning of a metonymic expression relies heavily on the context in which it is used. Understanding the intended meaning often requires considering the surrounding items or the specific situation. Metonymy involves mapping a source concept onto a target concept. This mapping occurs when a lexical item is used to represent a broader concept or when a lexical item is substituted with a closely related one. For example, the idiom *From the cradle to the grave* symbolizes a person's entire life, where *cradle* stands in for *birth* and *grave* for *death*. It signifies life from beginning to end. In *Boots on the ground*, the lexical item *boots* stands in for *soldiers*, indicating their physical presence in a military or police operation.

An example

As previously mentioned, metonymy is a form of figurative language in which a concept is referred to by the name of something closely associated with it. A common example of metonymy is when a place is used to represent an institution, industry or person. In the sentence *Westminster are trying to assess the event*, metonymy is used by replacing the name *Westminster* with *British government*, with which it is closely associated. This means that the British government is trying to assess the event. In this example, the abstract concept of place is understood in terms of the concrete concept of people. The literal interpretation of the sentence doesn't make sense because a place cannot assess an event, making it sound strange. However, the metonymic interpretation works well, with *Westminster* representing the *British government*. It is common for language users to refer to people by the place they live or work in. The metonymic mapping in this sentence provides a suitable context for understanding by linking the entities through a close conceptual relationship.

Patterns

As previously explained, metonymy is a cognitive phenomenon, not just a figure of speech, that plays a significant role in the organization of meaning. It involves substituting something for something else with which it is closely associated. In simple terms, it is when the name of an entity is replaced by the name of an attribute that it is connected to semantically. Metonymy is commonly used in spoken and written language, appearing on various levels of language structure and usage. It is carried out through the use of lexical items, with the most common process being the metonymic extension of a lexical item. Cognitive semanticists have identified three patterns of metonymy, each of which is described below.

Whole for part

This pattern involves using the whole of something to refer to part of it. The whole serves as a means of mentally accessing the part, allowing the whole to stand in for the part. Here are some examples of whole-for-part metonymies commonly found in everyday writing or conversation:

They eat *turkey* for Christmas dinner.	Turkey is used in place of meat.
The new *book* is highly informative.	The book is used in place of content.
The local *university* changed its mind.	University is used in place of staff.
The *windmill* built recently is turning.	The windmill is used in place of the vanes.
His *car* broke down on the main road.	The car is used in place of the engine.

Practice 11.1

State what each of the underlined lexical items stands for in the following ordinary sentences.

1. The knife made of metal is incredibly sharp.
2. He was the highest-paid editor in Fleet Street.
3. The top brass are reluctant to embrace change.
4. After his wife died, the man took to the bottle.
5. The White House released a further statement.

Part for whole

In this pattern, a part of something represents the whole. The part serves as a means to access the whole mentally. It is a cognitive process where two entities are linked so that the part symbolizes the whole. Here are some examples of part-for-whole metonymies used in everyday writing or conversation:

One set involves action:

She *authored* a book.	The agent (author) is a replacement for the action (writing).
He *hammered* the stone.	The instrument (hammer) is a replacement for the action (hitting).
She *peppered* the dish.	The object (pepper) is a replacement for the action (seasoning).
I *tiptoed* into the room.	The body part (tiptoe) is a replacement for the action (walking).
We *summered* at the resort.	Time (summer) is a replacement for the action (spending).

Another set involves causation:

The *Porsche* left without paying.	The object (Porsche) is a substitute for the user (driver).
I published a *paper* in the journal.	The material (paper) is a substitute for the object (article).
She received a *Picasso* as a reward.	The producer (Picasso) is a substitute for the product (painting).
The *redbreast* sang a sweet song.	The bodily feature (redbreast) is a substitute for the species (robin).
Alice is the *pride* of her college.	The passion (pride) is a substitute for the object inspiring it (person).

Practice 11.2

Discuss the types of metonymic relationships involved in the use of the underlined words in the examples below.

1. Shakespeare was England's <u>glory.</u>
2. I have read most of <u>Hardy.</u>
3. The <u>village</u> came out to greet him.
4. They are basking in the <u>sun.</u>
5. <u>Grey hairs</u> should be respected.

Symbol for symbolized

In this pattern, the name of a thing (symbol) is used to convey a certain idea or feeling (symbolized). The symbolized name has a close association with the related symbol. Here are some illustrative examples of symbol-symbolized metonymies used in everyday conversation:

She has always kept her *word*.	Word symbolizes promise.
That baby has all of my *heart*.	The heart symbolizes love.
Going down the hill is a *breeze*.	Breeze symbolizes ease.
He is always willing to lend a *hand*.	The hand symbolizes assistance.
It took a lot of *sweat* to achieve this.	Sweat symbolizes hard work.

Practice 11.3

In the examples below, write what each underlined lexical item symbolizes in the metonymic relationship.

1. Please, lend me your <u>ears</u>.
2. He has every right to the <u>sceptre</u>.
3. I spoke to her in her native <u>tongue</u>.
4. The <u>pen</u> is mightier than the <u>sword</u>.
5. The book describes her life from <u>cradle</u> to <u>grave</u>.

Advantages

The adoption of metonymic language in describing new experiences has provided practical advantages.

- Metonymy is a strategy for establishing reference by using the source domain to refer to an entity denoted by the target domain. This is represented by the stand-for notion. In *I filled the car up with petrol*, the word *car* is used to refer to the *tank*. This is a whole-part relationship, in which the whole *car* serves as a reference point for accessing the part, the *tank*. In *The violin is an excellent performer*, the word *violin* indirectly refers to the musician: the person who plays the violin. This relationship allows the part *violin* to serve as a reference point for accessing the musician.

- Metonymy is a technique for creating imagery by using language to evoke sensory experiences for the reader. In *The actor is a silver fox*, the phrase *silver fox* is used to describe an attractive middle-aged man with grey hair. The lexical items *silver* and *grey* create a vivid mental image. *Silver* means *grey* and *fox* means *good-looking*. In *The team needs some new blood*, the phrase *new blood* is used to symbolize new members joining the team, bringing an enlivening or stimulating effect. This language choice emphasizes strength, power and courage.

- Metonymy is a tool for making writing concise by avoiding word repetition and relying on word associations to emphasize the defining characteristics of a subject. By substituting one word for another, the writer gains the reader's attention and interest. In *We can leave the detailed negotiations to the suits*, the lexical item *suits* is used as metonymy for a business executive, reducing the description to its defining characteristic, the garment. A business executive refers to a person with an important job as a manager in a company or organization.

Summary

This chapter has outlined the general characteristics of the cognitive operation of metonymy. Metonymy is a cognitive process where one thing is used to refer to another. It often involves using a concrete concept to refer to something more complex or abstract. Metonymic thinking is an everyday process that is essential for making sense of the world and features in all forms of communication, serving a wide range of functions. In this process, there is a mapping between two things within the same domain where the qualities of one thing are figuratively mapped onto another. An object or concept is referred to not by its name, but by the name of something closely associated with it. As an important cognitive device, metonymy helps define abstract concepts using concrete ones, making it a major aspect of creativity in social interaction.

Key takeaways

- Metonymy is a cognitive device used to create imagery and convey meaning beyond the literal definition of lexical items.

- In metonymy, one object is named but another object is meant, with a certain association between them.

- Metonymy involves substituting one lexical item or phrase for another with which it is closely associated.

- Metonymy is subtle and flexible, often used by speakers when they do not wish to be entirely clear about a subject.

- Metonymy makes writing easy to understand, elegant and smooth, providing a concise way to communicate ideas or emotions.

Further reading

Metonymy as a cognitive phenomenon is discussed in Kövecses and Radden (1998), Panther and Radden (1999), Dirven and Pörings (2002), Croft (2006), Panther and Thornburg (2003, 2007), Peirsman and Geeraerts (2006), Barcelona (2015), Littlemore (2015) and Denroche (2015).

References

Barcelona, Antonio. 2015. Metonymy. In Ewa Dabrowska and Dagmar Divjak (eds.), *Handbook of Cognitive Linguistics*, 143–67. Berlin, München, Boston: De Gruyter Mouton.

Croft, William. 2006. The Role of Domains in the Interpretation of Metaphors and Metonymies. In Dirk Geeraerts (ed.), *Cognitive Linguistics: Basic Readings*, 269–302. Berlin: Mouton de Gruyter.

Denroche, Charles. 2015. *Metonymy and Language: A New Theory of Linguistic Processing*. London: Routledge.

Dirven, René and Ralph Pörings. 2002. *Metaphor and Metonymy in Comparison and Contrast*. Berlin: Mouton de Gruyter.

Kövecses, Zoltan and Günter Radden. 1998. Metonymy: Developing a Cognitive Linguistic View. *Cognitive Linguistics* 9 (1): 37–77.

Littlemore, Jeannette. 2015. *Metonymy: Hidden Shortcuts in Language, Thought and Communication*. Cambridge: Cambridge University Press.

Panther, Klaus-Uwe and Günter Radden. 1999. *Metonymy in Language and Thought*. Amsterdam: Benjamins.

Panther, Klaus-Uwe and Linda Thornburg. 2003. *Metonymy and Pragmatic Inferencing*. Amsterdam: John Benjamins.

Panther, Klaus-Uwe and Linda Thornburg. 2007. *Metonymy*. In Geeraerts and Cuyckens (eds.), *The Oxford Handbook of Cognitive Linguistics*, 236–63. Oxford: Oxford University Press.

Peirsman, Yves and Dirk Geeraerts. 2006. Metonymy as a Prototypical Category. *Cognitive Linguistics* 17 (3): 269–316.

CHAPTER TWELVE

The conceptual blending theory

Preview

This chapter explores the role of conceptual blending in meaning construction. **Conceptual blending**, also known as integration, is a mental operation that merges elements of two lexical items to form a new complex lexical item. The emergent structure has a unique meaning, while still retaining characteristics of the original elements. This process serves as a way to expand the vocabulary of a language. The goal is to demonstrate the importance of conceptual blending in the construction of meaning. The chapter is structured as follows. The first section serves as the introduction, discussing word formation and various processes, including blending. The second section delves into the theory of blending. The third section outlines the principles of the theory. The fourth section highlights the significant impact of the theory on lexical meaning. The fifth section enumerates the advantages of blending theory for lexical meaning. The final section summarizes the key concepts discussed in the chapter.

Introduction

One important aspect of most languages is word formation. This refers to the creation of new words through various processes such as derivation, compounding, abbreviation, acronym and blending. **Derivation** is the process of creating a word by adding a prefix or suffix to an existing root. For example, adding *dis-* to *agree* creates *disagree*, while adding *-dom* to *free* creates *freedom*. **Compounding** is the process of creating a word by adding up two or more different lexical items to create a new word with a meaning related to the original words. For example, combining *book* and *case* creates *bookcase*. **Abbreviation** is the process of creating a new word by either clipping part of the word or shortening it, such as *advertisement* to *ad*. Acronym involves using only the first letter(s) of each word, as in the United Nations becoming UN. The purpose of word formation is to expand vocabulary, enable the expression of new meanings and facilitate smooth communication.

Blending

Conceptual blending is essential to human thought and imagination, as it is a cognitive operation that creates new meanings. It involves blending two mental spaces to create a new space. The two spaces, called **input spaces**, represent relevant aspects of the concepts being combined, corresponding to the source and target domains of conceptual metaphor. The **blend**, also known as the created space or the blended space, emerges from the interaction of the input spaces, creating a unique meaning not found in either input alone. The blend incorporates information from both inputs but while adding additional details that are unique to the blend. There is also a generic space that helps identify counterparts in the input spaces, and serves as a foundation for shared information. In morphology, blending is a word-formation process that involves creating lexical items by combining parts of other lexical items. Morphological blends are a type of compounding, particularly seen in nominal compounds formed from adjective plus noun and noun plus noun combinations. Blending is a critical method for creating new lexical items in English.

Principles

- Input integration: Blending is considered a cognitive operation for creating new meanings, involving the combination of two or more mental spaces to form a new concept. This process occurs when inputs from different sources or cognitive domains are integrated to create a new structure that includes elements from each source. The integration process maps elements of the inputs into a blended space, where new connections and relationships can emerge, allowing for the integration of ideas and concepts that may not naturally coexist. This integration is reflected in the blend structure. For example, *canoodle* is a lexical item used to describe the action of paddling a canoe, demonstrating the result of integrating the two inputs *canoe* and *paddle*.

- Emergent structure: Meanings do not neatly fit into lexical items, but rather emerge during the meaning construction process. Viewing meaning as built rather than revealed allows analysts to focus on the process of integration rather than the end product. Therefore, blending is a creative process of meaning emergence where the integration of inputs and creation of new connections can lead to novel insights, interpretations or understandings. The emergent structure can develop into a complex mental representation separate from its original inputs. For example, the meaning of the lexical item *spork* is achieved through blending the two inputs *spoon* and *fork*, resulting in a spoon-shaped utensil with short tines at the tip.

- Cognitive motivation: Motivation is a central phenomenon in cognition, driving our ability to create and understand meaning by blending different concepts and ideas. The blending process is motivated by underlying cognitive and communicative needs. For example, the meaning of the lexical item *Brexit* is not arbitrary but motivated by conceptual integration or blending, a fundamental cognitive operation in the conceptual system crucial to human thought and imagination. *Brexit* refers to the British exit or withdrawal from the European Union, formally occurred on 31 January 2020. This example illustrates how elements and vital relations from diverse scenarios are blended in a subconscious process.

An example

As previously mentioned, blending is a form of figurative language in which meaning construction involves the selective integration of conceptual elements from two lexical items. A blend, in morphology, is a word formed from parts of two or more lexical items. Blending is a process of creating new words. A common example of blending is the lexical item *wheelchair*. Morphologically, it is composed of two input spaces *wheel*s, and *chair*. Semantically, certain core information from the input spaces is projected into the blended space *wheelchair*. The blend space links features from the input spaces to create a new blend. The emergent meaning of the blend, which goes beyond the meanings inherent in the two input spaces, is that of hospital or invalid or both. This and other blends have been so deeply established or entrenched that the language user no longer recognizes the blending background. As the example demonstrates, English is a dynamic language that is constantly evolving by combining parts to create new lexical items. It is an effective method used to increase vocabulary.

Patterns

As previously stated, blending is a cognitive phenomenon, not merely a figure of speech. It is a process of creating new lexical items, called blends, by combining parts of existing lexical items. A blend is a complex lexical item typically formed from two lexical fragments. Blending is very prevalent in both written and spoken language, and can be observed in language use and structure on various levels. It is facilitated by the use of lexical items. Blending is similar to compounding, with the key difference being that in blending part of one or both lexical items is omitted at the boundary between them. Blending is considered one of the most productive forms of word formation, generating valuable new words. From a morphological perspective, cognitive semanticists identify three patterns of blending. Below is a description of each pattern.

Initial + final

In this pattern, the initial part of one lexical item is combined with the final part of another item to create a unique lexical item with a new meaning. Here are some examples of blends:

smog	(smoke + fog)'
motel	(motor + hotel)
brunch	(breakfast + lunch)
motorcade	(motor + cavalcade)
camcorder	(camera + recorder)

Practice 12.1

Describe in detail the conceptual blends in each of the following morphological formulations.

1. globish
2. telegenic
3. blizzaster
4. boxercise
5. sportscast

Initial + initial

In this pattern, the beginning of one lexical item is combined with the beginning of another item, creating a unique lexical item with a new meaning. Here are some examples of blends:

telex   teleprinter + exchange)
moped   (motor + pedal)
sitcom   (situation + comedy)
internet (international + network)
cyborg   (cybernetic + organism)

Practice 12.2

Identify the lexical items out of which the following morphological blends are formulated.

1. vlog
2. email
3. biopic
4. romcom
5. frenemy

whole + part

In this pattern, a complete lexical item is merged with a portion of another lexical item to form a new lexical item with a distinct meaning. Here are a few examples of blends:

chillax   (chill + relax)
webinar   (web + seminar)
newscast   (news + broadcast)
videophone   (video + telephone)
breathalyser   (breath + analyser)

Practice 12.3

In each of the following morphological formulations, explain in detail how the blends are formed.

1. fanzine
2. mocktail
3. staycation
4. workaholic
5. dumbfound

Advantages

The adoption of blending language in describing new experiences has provided practical advantages.

- Blending helps facilitate communication by allowing speakers to shorten their message and convey it quickly. This productive process enables speakers to combine two or more ideas or lexical items into one coherent item in a matter of moments. For example, instead of saying I sent the message by *electronic mail*, one can say I sent the message by *email*. Similarly, instead of saying *The car has a traffic indicator*, one can say *The car has a trafficator*, which is a blinking light on a motor vehicle used to indicate a change of direction.

- Blending offers language users a way of describing new experiences by combining information from two different spaces to create a novel blend. This process plays a vital role in adding new lexical items to the lexicon through the creation of new lexical items. For instance, combining the lexical items *food* and *alcoholic* results in the blend *foodoholic*, which refers to a lover of food, or a foodie. Similarly, blending the lexical items *friend* and *family* gives us *framily*, which describes a group of friends who are as close as a family.

- Blending is a tool used to coin new inventions and modern trends, often employed in the fields of mass media, technological developments and commercial advertisements. Lexical blends serve as attention-catching linguistic devices. For instance, the blend *cinaplex* combines *cinema* and *complex*, referring to a cinema with multiple screens. Another example is the blend *malware*, formed from *malicious* and *software*, describing software intended to harm or disable computers and systems.

Summary

This chapter has explored the role of blends in constructing meaning. Blending aims to establish a shared model of the meaning-making process and the emergence of new concepts. It is a common occurrence in human thought, reflected in everyday language. Blending is a dynamic process where structures from two input mental spaces are projected into a third space, the blend. It involves mapping between different spaces to create a blend, combining materials from two distinct sources. The integration of two elements into a single unit is a key motivation behind blending, making it a powerful cognitive tool essential for language and communication. The elements from the input spaces that enter the blend are called projections, which can take various patterns. Overall, blending offers a clear explanation of creativity through the emergent structure it produces.

Key takeaways

- Blending involves integrating inputs from different sources to create a new structure. The new structure incorporates elements from each source and takes on a different meaning.
- The integration process involves mapping, where elements from different sources are matched up with each other. This mapping allows for the blending of ideas and concepts that may not naturally go together.
- Blending often results in the emergence of a new structure and meaning. By integrating inputs and forming new connections, novel insights, interpretations or understandings can arise.
- Blending is motivated by cognitive and communicative needs. This motivation fuels our ability to generate and comprehend meaning by blending different concepts and ideas.
- Blending is widely applicable across various domains of human cognition and communication. It is a strategy used to facilitate communication and foster creative thinking.

Further reading

The concept of blending is addressed in Oakley (1998), Grady, Oakley and Coulson (1999), Gibbs (2000), Coulson and Oakley (2000), Coulson (2001), Fauconnier and Turner (1996, 2002), Radden (2009), Janda (2011) and Turner (2014).

References

Coulson, Seana. 2001. *Semantic Leaps: Frame-shifting and Conceptual Blending in Meaning*. Cambridge: Cambridge University Press.
Coulson, Seana and Todd Oakley (eds.), 2000. Blending Basics. *Cognitive Linguistics* 11 (3/4): 175–96.
Fauconnier, Gilles and Mark Turner. 1996. Blending as a Central Process of Grammar. In A. Goldberg (ed.), *Conceptual Structure, Discourse, and Language*, 113–130. Stanford, CA: Center for the Study of Language and Information.

Fauconnier, Gilles and Mark Turner. 2002. *The Way We Think: Conceptual Blending and the Mind's Hidden Complexities*. New York: Basic Books.
Gibbs, Raymond, 2000. Making Good Psychology out of Blending Theory. *Cognitive Linguistics* 11 (3/4): 347–58.
Grady, Joseph, Todd Oakley and Seana Coulson. 1999. Blending and Metaphor. In R. W. Gibbs and G. Steen (eds.), *Metaphor in Cognitive Linguistics*, 101–24. Amsterdam: John Benjamins.
Janda, Laura. 2011. Metonymy in Word-formation. *Cognitive Linguistics* 22-2, 359– 392.
Oakley, Todd, 1998. Conceptual Blending, Narrative Discourse, and Rhetoric. *Cognitive Linguistics* 9: 321–60.
Radden, Günter. 2009. Generic Reference in English: A Metonymic and Conceptual Blending Analysis. In Klaus-Uwe Panther, Linda Thornburg, Antonio Barcelona (eds.), *Metonymy and Metaphor in Grammar*, 199–228. Amsterdam: John Benjamins.
Turner, Mark. 2014. *The Origin of Ideas: Blending, Creativity, and the Human Spark*. New York: Oxford University Press.

C

Usage mechanisms

In the generative approach, language is viewed as a set of innate syntactic rules that govern the language system. This approach provides rules for existing patterns and assists speakers in creating new ones. It clearly distinguishes between knowledge of language and the actual use of language, separating the language faculty from cognitive influence, thus excluding the speaker's role in shaping language. The focus is more on competence (abstract linguistic knowledge) rather than performance (actual language usage). In contrast, the cognitive approach does not see language as a rule-driven system. Language is seen as a collection of form-meaning mappings, where a wide variety of conventional emerge through usage. In other words, language users in a speech community establish conventional units and produce specific linguistic patterns. A language pattern becomes a conventional unit when it is used and understood frequently to convey a particular idea.

Effects

- Frequency: This refers to how a linguistic structure becomes a cognitive pattern or routine in an individual language user's mind through repeated use. The more frequently a particular linguistic structure is used, the more likely it is entrenched in the language user's mind, influencing the language user's perception of how salient or obvious particular structures are.
- Conventionalization: This is the process by which conventions (established linguistic patterns) are formed. Through repeated use, certain linguistic structures become conventionalized or standardized

within a language community, becoming shared knowledge, and leading thus to the formation of patterns and rules.

- Creativity: This is the capacity of the human mind to generate and comprehend a seemingly endless variety of previously undiscovered linguistic structures. New linguistic structures emerge through innovative language use, making language use a creative endeavour. Language users are more motivated, inspired or challenged when they can produce something new.

- Context: This refers to the linguistic and situational context in which a lexical item is used. Context is crucial in determining the meaning of lexical items, as they are used differently depending on social and pragmatic circumstances. Without context, language cannot effectively serve as a means of communication.

- Analogy: This is the cognitive process of comparing one thing to another based on discernible similarities. Speakers create new expressions by drawing on established patterns stored in their minds. When identifying a structurally similar pattern, the speaker can extend the analogy by predicting other patterns.

CHAPTER THIRTEEN

The usage-based theory

Preview

This chapter explores the application of the usage-based theory to the semantic characterization of lexical items. **Usage-based** posits that usage has an effect on linguistic structure, suggesting that language units emerge from specific usage events. The goal is to explain the emergence of linguistic structure from language use, with the idea that the grammar in the mind of the speaker is shaped by usage and emerges from actual language use. The chapter is organized as follows. The first section serves as the introduction, discussing two opposing theories of language acquisition. The universal grammar-based theory suggests that knowledge of language comes from an innate system of rules, where grammar generates language use. In contrast, the usage-based theory proposes that knowledge of language results from language use, with language use generating grammar. The second section presents the usage-based theory. The third section emphasizes the claims of the theory. The fourth section demonstrates the application of the theory. The fifth section lists the benefits of the usage-based theory and evaluates its viability. The final section summarizes the main points of the chapter.

Introduction

The ability to acquire and use language is a key aspect that distinguishes humans from other beings. Language acquisition is the process by which humans gain the ability to understand and produce language. A major debate in understanding language acquisition is how language users pick up the ability from linguistic input. Scholars fall into two groups of thought on this matter. One group follows the universal grammar-based theory, which is part of generative grammar. This theory argues that grammar is the fundamental component of language production, with pragmatics and lexicon serving grammar. Generative linguists believe that the mind has a specific module for language acquisition and that grammar originates from an innate blueprint, rather than being entirely inductive. The other group follows the usage-based theory, which is part of Cognitive Grammar. This theory argues that grammar is produced through language use, with language structure evolving based on experience rather than rules. In brief, whereas the generative theory emphasizes the existence of rules, the cognitive theory focuses on the influence of experience in language acquisition.

Usage-based theory

The usage-based theory of language emerged in the late 1980s as a reaction against formal trends in linguistics that viewed language as a static and isolated system. This theory, as Langacker argues, sees language structure as a result and function of real language use, with new uses shaping how the linguistic system will develop. This theory takes a maximalist, non-reductive and bottom-up approach to analysing linguistic structure. **Maximalist** means it addresses all aspect of language, not just certain levels of representation. **Non-reductionist** means it lists specific and general patterns. **Bottom-up** means that general patterns emerge from specific ones. This approach implies the redundancy and complexity of grammar. Language is viewed as a dynamic system of emergent symbolic units and flexible restrictions shaped by cognitive processes involved in language use. Language development is significantly influenced by the language user's experience with specific linguistic elements.

Claims

- Language is grounded in its use. **Use** refers to the act of employing a lexical item for its intended purpose. The meaning of a lexical item is derived from how it is used in a particular context. The context in which a lexical item is used is the best evidence available for accounting for its interpretation. The use of context has an important consequence as it helps to account for lexical meaning. A lexical item has not only a conventional meaning, known as a coded meaning, but also a contextual meaning, known as a pragmatic meaning. Lexical items are not defined by reference to the objects they designate or by the mental representations one might associate with them, but by how they are used. The meaning of a lexical item is what it expresses or represents. For example, the sentence *He uncovered the thing* has two interpretations. When uttered by an official, it is likely to mean 'discover something secret', as in *He uncovered the plot*. When uttered by a mother, it is likely to mean 'remove the cover from something', as in *She uncovered the pan*. The examples demonstrate that context interacts with the speaker's intention and plays a crucial role in how the utterance is interpreted by the hearer.

- Language is determined by its usage. **Usage** refers to the way a lexical item is commonly used in language. Language is acquired through actual usage, rather than being solely governed by innate grammatical rules. Linguistic structure, whether lexical or grammatical, is largely a product of the speakers' collective and accumulated experience. For example, *Can I go to the party?* is not ideal when one is seeking permission. The reason is that *can* implies a physical ability to do so. Likewise, *May I go to the party?* is not ideal when one is talking about physical ability. The reason is that *may* implies asking for permission. As these examples show, the meanings of lexical items are deeply connected to their usage within a given language. This principle is of paramount importance in understanding language and communication. Language units are form-meaning pairings produced by cognitive processes, human abilities that relate and integrate the units in various ways. The units are recognized by, and accessible to, others in the linguistic community. This stems from the basic insight that language usage has a constant effect on language structure, meaning that language structure is inseparable from its usage.

- Language is dynamic. It is continuously evolving rather than being static and prescriptive. The linguistic system is derived from **utterances**, actual instances of language use. These instances represent situated **usage events**, specific utterances of language use, employed to convey particular meanings. In the usage-based model, usage events are seen as crucial to understanding how language works, as they provide insight into how grammar and meaning are intertwined. They serve as a window into understanding language, focusing on how linguistic expressions are linked to their contexts of use and the cognitive processes that underlie their production and comprehension. For example, consider the lexical item *look*. In different usage events, it can take on various meanings. In *I am looking for my keys*, it means to search for something. In *The sunset looks beautiful*, it conveys the idea of appearance. In *She gave me a dirty look*, it implies a facial expression conveying disapproval or anger. These examples demonstrate how the same lexical item can be used in different ways to convey a range of meanings in distinct usage events.

- Language is bipolar. Its structure and substance are tightly linked through the concept of construal. Construal refers to how linguistic forms express conceptualizations of various situations, actions and events. The structure refers to the phonological form, whereas the substance refers to the semantic content. Both are related via language use, which is in turn influenced by experience. The linkage is important since the intent of the speaker in employing a particular form is to convey a particular meaning. Any linguistic unit, lexical or grammatical, is meaningful and its structure reflects its substance. In this respect, the linguistic alternatives available to the speaker are not on an equal footing. They are motivated by semantic considerations, which include clues from both linguistic and non-linguistic worlds. For example, consider the difference between the verbs *give* and *receive*. The form of each verb carries inherent meaning. The form of *give* implies a voluntary transfer of possession or control, while the form of *receive* suggests an involuntary acquisition of something. This interplay between form and meaning demonstrates how linguistic structures are not arbitrary but are grounded in conceptualizations of human experience.

- Meaning is embedded in culture. The usage-based theory takes language to be an embodied and social human behaviour. It refers to the idea that the way we interpret and understand the world is heavily influenced by the cultural context in which we exist. Our language, traditions, beliefs and societal norms all play a significant role in shaping our perceptions and interpretations of the world around us. Definitions of lexical items emerge from the culture and society in which they are used. Wittgenstein stresses the social aspects of cognition; to see how language works in most cases, we have to see how it functions in a specific social situation. Understanding that meaning is grounded in culture is essential for effective cross-cultural communication, as it allows us to recognize and appreciate the diversity of perspectives and interpretations that exist in the world. Take the lexical item *cool*, for instance, it can have different connotations in different social groups. In a group of teenagers, *cool* might mean something trendy or impressive, while in a group of older adults, it might simply mean a comfortable temperature.

Applications

Of special interest in this work is the usage-based study of lexis. Lexical items play a crucial role in this theory as it examines how they are learned, used and adapted in different contexts based on their patterns of usage. The theory also considers how the usage of lexical items contributes to language acquisition and overall language proficiency. Therefore, lexical items are an important aspect of the usage-based theory of language as they reflect the way language is used and learned in real-life communication. This theory recognizes the significance of lexical items in shaping language development and use. On this account, the power of lexical items is inextricably linked to their usage, showing how language users creatively apply and adapt their language use based on their linguistic experiences and the communicative needs of different contexts. In other words, the theory sheds light on how linguistic choices are influenced by the context of communication and the individuals involved.

Usage-based linguistics can account for two types of language variation: intraspeaker and interspeaker. Variation within the language of a single speaker is called **intraspeaker variation**, where the alternation between lexical items is constrained by the linguistic context in which they occur. Variation between languages is called **interspeaker variation**, where the alternation between lexical items is constrained by the cultural context in which they occur. Variation is inherent in human language: a single speaker will use different linguistic forms on different occasions, and different speakers of a language will express the same meanings using different forms. Understanding intraspeaker and interspeaker variations is crucial in the field of sociolinguistics as it helps researchers and language experts analyse and appreciate the different factors that influence language use and variation within and across speech communities. Cultural variation can influence aspects such as vocabulary, speech patterns and even non-verbal communication, all of which contribute to the overall understanding of interspeaker variation.

Intraspeaker variations

Intraspeaker variation refers to the variation in an individual speaker's language use over time or across different contexts. This type of variation occurs within the same speaker. Intraspeaker variations encompass stylistic variations in lexical items. According to the usage-based theory, language use shapes and determines the structure of language. Stylistic variations in lexical items can be observed through the way language users adapt their choice of lexical items to fit different contexts. It can be seen when a person switches between formal and informal language based on the social context. That is, an individual may use different styles or registers of language depending on the setting. For example, in formal writing, people may use lexical items such as *cease* instead of *stop*. In informal conversations, individuals may use *gonna* instead of *going to* to express future actions. These examples demonstrate how usage-based theory helps explain how people's usage of language or choice of lexical items varies based on different contexts.

Formal language is official and academic, whereas informal language is casual and spontaneous.

Here are sample lists of examples of lexical items with both formal and informal varieties.

verbs
Formal:	repair	endeavour	prohibit	liberate	reside
Informal:	fix	try	ban	free	live

Adjectives
Formal:	insane	intelligent	vacant	entire	difficult
Informal:	mad	smart	empty	whole	tough

Nouns
Formal:	notion	opportunity	vision	demise	occupation
Informal:	idea	chance	sight	death	job

Practice 13.1

Indicate how the following informal lexical items are expressed or lexically replaced in formal English.

1. ask 2. book 3. check 4. get 5. need
6. help 7. keep 8. tell 9. let 10. fight

Interspeaker variations

Interspeaker variation refers to the differences in language use among different speakers or groups of speakers. These variations are often caused by differences in culture. The meaning of a lexical item can change depending on the cultural context in which it is used. Some lexical items may have different meanings in different cultures, which can sometimes lead to misunderstandings, especially when the lexical items can be interpreted positively or negatively. These misunderstandings often stem from differences in the cultural background of the speakers. Interspeaker variation can also be seen in the different dialects or accents spoken by individuals from various regions. Additionally, it can be attributed to the use of expressions that are specific to a particular community or culture, showcasing the linguistic diversity among speakers. For example, some people may use the term *auntie* or *aunty* to refer to their female parent's sister, while others may use the term *aunt*. These variations in lexical usage are influenced by the different ways in which language is used in everyday interactions.

Here are some illustrative examples of adjectives with positive and negative connotations, representing cultural variations.

fat
thin
loud
reserved
aggressive

The lexical items mentioned above are interpreted differently depending on the cultural norms of a particular society, specifically the cultural background of the speaker and listener. In some cultures, these items may have a negative connotation, whereas in others they may be viewed as a positive trait. In some cultures, they may be seen as a compliment, while in others they may be considered as insult. For instance, in some cultures being *thin* is often associated with beauty and health, while in others it may be seen as a sign of illness or poverty. Similarly, the adjective *loud* may be perceived as a sign of confidence and assertiveness, while in others it may be seen as rude or obnoxious. Therefore, it is important to be mindful of cultural differences when using adjectives in communication. It is important to consider the context in which the adjective is being used and to be aware of the potential for misinterpretation. By being sensitive to cultural nuances, we can ensure that our communication is effective and respectful. These examples highlight the significance of understanding cultural differences and language subtleties when interacting with individuals from diverse backgrounds.

Practice 13.2

Each of the following adjectives can be viewed positively or negatively, depending on the cultural context.

1. old
2. lofty
3. polite
4. cheap
5. extravagant

Advantages

The usage-based model of language has several advantages, each of which can be exemplified through the lens of lexical items.

- In the usage-based model, language is seen as flexible and adaptive, allowing for the incorporation of new lexical items based on their frequency of use. For instance, consider the lexical item *google* which, due to its common usage as a verb meaning to search for something online, has been incorporated into many languages besides English.

- The usage-based model emphasizes the importance of context in language use, allowing for more nuanced and effective understanding of lexical items. For example, the lexical item *flight* has two different meanings: a plane journey, and the act of running away. The difference appears in use. This follows from the basic insight that usage has an effect on meaning.

- The usage-based model recognizes the dynamic nature of language, allowing for the evolution and adaptation of lexical items to new situations. For instance, the lexical item *tweet* primarily refers to the sound of a bird, but now commonly refers to a message posted on the social media platform Twitter, reflecting the evolving nature of language.

- The usage-based model focuses on how language is actually used in real-life situations, making it highly practical and enhancing the practical application of lexical items. For instance, the lexical item *app*, short for *application*, has become widely used to refer to software on mobile devices, reflecting its practical application in modern technology.

Overall, the usage-based model of language offers a more practical and flexible approach to understanding and using language, aligning with the way that language functions in the real world.

Summary

In this chapter, I emphasized the role of usage as a key shaper of meaning in language. Knowledge of actual usage is the foundation of language knowledge. In a usage-based theory of language, the complexity of language at all levels emerges not as a result of a language-specific instinct but through the interaction of cognition and use. Language is not simply a set of abstract rules and structures, but is heavily influenced by how it is actually used in real communication. This theory highlights the impact of usage patterns on language acquisition and development, suggesting that learners acquire language through exposure to and interaction with language in meaningful contexts. The use and interpretation of lexical items are influenced by linguistic and cultural differences, which play a significant role as the meanings of lexical items can vary depending on the linguistic and cultural contexts in which they are used. To avoid misinterpretations, it is essential to be aware of the nuances of lexical items in order to effectively communicate and connect with people from different backgrounds.

Key takeaways

- Language is not just a set of rules and structures, but is heavily influenced by usage in real communication.
- Language learning and usage are closely connected, as learners acquire language through exposure to and interaction with language in meaningful contexts.
- Language is adaptable and constantly evolving based on how it is used in different contexts and by different speakers.
- Language acquisition and proficiency are shaped by the frequency and usage patterns that an individual experiences.
- Language structure emerges from language use. Actual language use is a primary shaper of linguistic form.

Further Reading

There is a handful of references on the usage-based theory and its application to various aspects of language. I suggest the following works for further reading: Langacker (1988, 2000), Bybee (2010, 2023), Tomasello (2003), Kemmer and Barlow (2000), Diessel (2017), and Díaz-Campos and Balasch (2023). These works present a clear and detailed account of the ideas introduced in the usage-based theory of language.

References

Bybee, Joan. 2023. What Is Usage-based Linguistics? In Manuel Díaz-Campos and Sonia Balasch (eds.). *The Handbook of Usage-Based Linguistics*. New Jersey, NJ: John Wiley & Sons.

Bybee, Joan and Clay Beckner. 2010. Usage-based Theory. In B. Heine and H. Narrog (eds.), *The Oxford Handbook of Linguistic Analysis*, 827–56. Oxford: Oxford University Press.

Díaz-Campos, Manuel and Sonia Balasch (eds.). 2023. *The Handbook of Usage-based Linguistics*. New Jersey, NJ: John Wiley & Sons, Inc.

Diessel, Holgar. 2017. Usage-based Linguistics. In Mark Aronoff (ed.), *Oxford Research Encyclopedia of Linguistics*. New York: Oxford University Press.

Kemmer, Suzanne and Michael Barlow (eds.). 2000. *Usage-based Models of Language*. Stanford: Center for the Study of Language and Information.

Langacker, Ronald. 1988. A Usage-based Model. In B. Rudzka-Ostyn (ed.), *Topics in Cognitive Linguistics*, 127–61. Amsterdam: John Benjamins.

Langacker, Ronald. 2000. A Dynamic Usage-based Model. In M. Barlow and S. Kemmer (eds.), *Usage-based Models of Language*, 24–63. Stanford: Stanford University.

Tomasello, Michael. (2003). *Constructing a Language: A Usage-based Theory of Language Acquisition*. Cambridge, MA: Harvard University Press.

Conclusions

Preview

This study has dealt with lexical meaning in English. Meaning is the semantic content associated with a symbol, represented by a linguistic form. Various theories have emerged to tackle lexical meaning. The traditional approach (word-to-world) suggests that the meaning of a lexical item refers to things and situations in the world. The structural approach (word-to-word) posits that the meaning of a lexical item is derived from the network of its relations with other items. The generative approach (word-to-content) breaks down the meaning of a lexical item into primitive components. The cognitive approach (world-to-word) views the meaning of a lexical item as a concept in the mind, grounded in perception and experience. This book adopts the cognitive approach, known as Cognitive Lexical Semantics. The analysis is based on its assumptions and employs its tools effectively to understand lexical meaning.

Cognitive Lexical Semantics has proposed some theories based on viable assumptions for analysing lexical meaning rigorously and efficiently. These theories offer insights into language, meaning, human mind, and the relationship between language and cognition. They explain how lexical meaning is produced and understood, showing that language is meaning and meaning is conceptualization. The key idea is that meaning is rooted in experience, linguistic knowledge is conceptual and semantic structures are based on general cognitive capacities. This suggests that linguistic and non-linguistic structures share fundamental sensory characteristics at the representational level.

Theoretical contributions

The textbook is theoretically based on cognitive assumptions throughout the analysis and has made three contributions.

Lexical multiplicity

The first theoretical contribution that Cognitive Lexical Semantics has made to the area of lexical meaning is shown by the use of the cognitive tenet of category. According to this tenet, lexical items are polysemous; they contain peripheral zones that gather around clear centres, i.e. the prototype. Any lexical item is argued to form a category of distinct but related senses, both prototypical and peripheral. The prototype of the category has the key properties of the category. It is the sense that comes to mind first or is the easiest to recall. The periphery of the category contains the remaining senses, regular and irregular, which are linked to the prototype via meaning extensions. The peripheral senses have some, but not all, of the properties of the category. The peripheral senses inherit the specifications of the category, but flesh out the category in contrasting ways. They exhibit overlapping semantic nuances. This view opposes the traditional view, which describes the various senses of a lexical item as discrete, well-defined entities that can be strictly separated from each other.

Lexical specificity

The second theoretical contribution that Cognitive Lexical Semantics has made to the area of lexical meaning is shown by the use of the cognitive tenet of frame. Given this tenet, the meanings of lexical items can best be described relative to the frame to which they belong. A frame is a knowledge structure in terms of which the exact role or the specialized status of a lexical item can be defined. It is a context of background knowledge about which the specific meanings of lexical items are identified. The lexical items of a language have interlocking senses such that to understand the meaning of any item it is necessary to understand the properties of the frame in which it occurs, as well as the properties of the other members of the frame. A frame represents a concept in which different types of relationships are held between its members. The relationships are defined in terms of minimally divergent semantic roles. Each member fits one aspect of the frame which is precisely different from the other. This view contrasts with the traditional view, which describes the meanings of lexical items in isolation.

Lexical alternation

The third theoretical contribution that Cognitive Lexical Semantics has made to the area of lexical meaning is demonstrated by the use of the cognitive principle of construal. It is argued that the choice of a lexical item is correlated with the particular construal imposed on a situation. Construal is a cognitive ability that allows the speaker to conceptualize a situation in different ways and select the appropriate lexical structures to represent them in discourse. According to this principle, no two lexical items are synonymous. Upon closer examination, it becomes clear that they are not identical in meaning or interchangeable in use. The two lexical items represent different conceptualizations of the same situation. These different conceptualizations are a reflection of the speaker's varied mental experiences. This implies that two lexical items may have the same conceptual content, but differ in the construal imposed on that content. Each lexical item is suitable for a specific situation, and therefore the alternatives available to the speaker should not be considered equal. This stance contrasts sharply with the traditional view, which treats seemingly similar lexical items as synonymous.

Methodical contributions

This textbook has methodically used cognitive tools throughout the analysis and made five contributions.

Meaning is flexible

The first methodical contribution achieved by the textbook in the field of lexical meaning is the flexibility of lexical meaning. The way lexical items work is flexible and analogous, a result of the discriminating contexts in which the lexical items appear. Context is the environment in which a lexical item is used, providing the background knowledge against which a lexical item is produced and understood. Context also plays a role in disambiguating the meaning of a lexical item, relating to the other elements in an utterance that precede or follow it. The potential context in which a lexical item appears is a response to the communicative needs of the discourse, with each lexical item having a contextual preference. Therefore, the meaning of a lexical item can only be derived from the context in which it occurs, making context the best evidence available in accounting for interpretation. Context interacts with the speaker's intention and plays a crucial role in how a lexical item is interpreted by the hearer. This view is a reaction against the traditional view in which lexical items function in a rigid, algorithmic fashion.

Meaning is encyclopaedic

The second methodical contribution that the textbook has achieved in the field of lexical meaning is the encyclopaedic nature of meaning. The meaning of a lexical item encompasses two types of knowledge. One is dictionary knowledge, which pertains to linguistic meaning. The other is encyclopaedic knowledge, which pertains to general knowledge. Dictionary knowledge relates to understanding what lexical items mean. The dictionary meaning is the direct referential, denotative meaning of a lexical item. Encyclopaedic knowledge, on the other hand, relates to a general understanding of the world. Encyclopaedic knowledge is not directly related to linguistic knowledge. The encyclopaedic meaning refers to the indirect, non-referential, connotative meaning of a lexical item. Language does not encode meaning, instead, lexical items provide access to a vast inventory of structured knowledge. This encyclopaedic knowledge is grounded in human interaction with others (social experience) and the world around us (physical experience). An encyclopaedia is thus an information bank. This stance contradicts the traditional view, which argues that lexical definitions should be separated from encyclopaedic information.

Meaning is non-autonomous

The third methodical contribution that the textbook has achieved in the field of lexical meaning is the non-autonomy of meaning. The study of lexical meaning is an integral part of human cognition, dependent on the cognitive organization of the human mind. Language is an experiential phenomenon closely tied to general cognitive processes. Lexical meaning can only be understood in the context of human cognitive abilities. Language is a cognitive tool for expressing human experience, which is unique to each individual user. This suggests that lexical meaning must consider the experiential background of the language user. Lexical meaning revolves around how language users interact with the world. The meaning that language users derive from and through language is not a separate and independent module of the mind, but rather reflects overall experience. Social and cultural environments influence lexical meaning. Lexical items do not exist in isolation; they are always part of actual utterances produced by humans. This stance contrasts with the traditional view, which separates the study of semantic phenomena from context-specific information.

Meaning is distinctive

The fourth methodical contribution that the textbook has made in the field of lexical meaning is the semantic distinction between lexical items. A semantic distinction occurs when two lexical items appear in the same context but have different meanings. These two lexical items are not freely interchangeable, so it is improper to use one for the other without consideration. They are in complementary distribution, meaning that one can be found in one environment and the other in a different environment. Each lexical item serves a unique purpose in communication. If a context accepts two lexical items, it has two meanings and thus two resulting structures. The book explored this doctrine to explain lexical pairs, arguing that such pairs have the same content but represent two different conceptualizations. Each lexical item describes the same situation, but does so in its own way. The choice between them is a function of meaning. In each conceptualization, the speaker opts for a different item, as a different item is associated with a different nuance of meaning. This stance contradicts with the traditional view, which considers seemingly similar lexical items as synonymous.

Meaning is compatible

The fifth methodical contribution that the textbook has made in the field of lexical meaning is semantic compatibility or collocationality, which is the tendency of lexical items to occur together in a language. Lexical items do not combine freely in utterances. Instead, they combine naturally with some items and less naturally with others. The combination is governed by the semantic compatibility between them. Viewing an utterance as a meaningful template imposes constraints of semantic compatibility between its meaning and that of each of its internal elements. In cognitive terms, this is referred to as **correspondence**: the compatibility between two substructures in forming a composite structure. For example, the adjective *thick* is compatible with both *fog* and *soup*, but only *dense* is compatible with *fog*. The distribution of the phrase *dense fog* is the result of the semantic compatibility that exists between the lexical items in the phrase. This stance contradicts with the traditional view, which explains restrictions in terms of features belonging to one lexical item versus features belonging to another.

APPENDICES

What is the difference between Cognitive Lexical Semantics and formal Lexical Semantics?

Cognitive Lexical Semantics and formal Lexical Semantics are two approaches used to study the meaning of lexical items and their relationships within a language. While both approaches contribute to our understanding of language meaning, the way they approach the field differs in several ways:

- Cognitive Lexical Semantics grounds the study of meaning in mental capacities. It takes a cognitive and psychological perspective, aiming to understand how meaning is stored, processed and represented in the human mind. In comparison, formal Lexical Semantics grounds the study of meaning in mathematical rules. It is more concerned with developing formal systems and mathematical models to represent and analyse lexical meaning.

- Cognitive Lexical Semantics often relies on introspective data, experimental research and psychological evidence to substantiate theoretical claims. It may also involve corpus linguistics, examining large bodies of naturally occurring language data. In contrast, formal Lexical Semantics primarily relies on logical and mathematical formalisms for analysis, and often uses natural language corpora to extract meaning representations.

- Cognitive Lexical Semantics often uses network models such as semantic networks or spreading activation models to analyse and understand meaning, attaching specific importance to context and conceptual knowledge. By contrast, formal Lexical Semantics uses formal representations such as logical formulas, lambda calculi or semantic feature structures to analyse and understand meaning, often divorced from context.

- Cognitive Lexical Semantics pays attention to various lexical relationships, and explores how these relationships are represented and processed in the mind. It considers the dynamic nature of meaning and the influence of context in shaping these relationships. Formal Lexical Semantics also studies lexical relationships but often uses mathematical operations, set theory or formal logic to establish precise rules and interpretations.

- Cognitive Lexical Semantics is often applied to the fields of psycholinguistics, cognitive science, natural language processing or machine translation systems, focusing on how meaning is processed and interpreted by language users. Formal Lexical Semantics, on the other hand, is more commonly applied in computational linguistics, natural language understanding and knowledge representation tasks that require formal reasoning and analysis of meaning.

What makes Cognitive Lexical Semantics different from other lexical approaches to language?

Cognitive Lexical Semantics is a linguistic approach that focuses on the relationship between language and human cognition. It seeks to understand how meaning is constructed and represented in the mind, and how it is expressed through language. Here are some key ways in which Cognitive Lexical Semantics differs from other approaches:

- Cognitive Lexical Semantics emphasizes the importance of embodied experiences in shaping meaning. It recognizes that meaning arises from direct experiences with the world. This leads to the adoption of metaphor, metonymy, image schema, mental spaces and blending. This stands in contrast to other approaches that focus solely on linguistic structures and formal rules.

- Cognitive Lexical Semantics draws heavily on prototype theory, whereby meanings are formed based on typical or representative examples of a category. It emphasizes graded membership within categories, where some instances are more prototypical than others. This differs from other approaches, which often rely on categorical definitions and strict boundaries.

- Cognitive Lexical Semantics explores the role of metaphor in shaping our understanding of language and thought. It argues that metaphors are not just rhetorical devices but fundamental cognitive mechanisms that structure our conceptual systems. This differs from other approaches that may view metaphor as a more superficial linguistic phenomenon.

- Cognitive Lexical Semantics recognizes the importance of context in influencing meaning. It highlights how different aspects of the context such as the speaker's intentions, discourse environment and situational factors can impact the interpretation of lexical items. Other approaches may focus more narrowly on the syntactic or semantic properties of language.

- Cognitive Lexical Semantics takes a usage-based perspective, which emphasizes the role of actual language use in influencing meaning. It views language as a dynamic system that is constantly evolving through usage and interaction. This stands in contrast to other approaches that emphasize fixed grammatical rules and structures in the study of meaning.

Overall, Cognitive Lexical Semantics offers a more holistic and dynamic view of language and meaning, incorporating insights from cognitive psychology, neuroscience and linguistics. It puts a strong emphasis on the role of cognition and embodiment in shaping linguistic expressions and their interpretation.

What is the difference between universal grammar-based model and usage-based model of language?

Both the universal grammar-based model and usage-based model aim to explain how humans acquire and use language. They both recognize the importance of cognitive processes in language learning and use. However, there are key differences between the two models:

- The universal grammar-based model, proposed by Noam Chomsky, suggests that humans have an innate, pre-programmed set of linguistic principles that shape language structures. According to this model, grammar is governed by universal principles, hardwired into the human brain from birth. On the other hand, the usage-based model, proposed by Ronald Langacker, focuses on how language use shapes language structure. This model emphasizes the impact of language use and social interaction on language development.

- In the universal grammar-based model, language is rule-dependent, with rules generating grammatical sentences and assigning structural descriptions. In contrast, the usage-based model is schema-dependent, with grammar consisting of conventional units organized by schema-instance relations. A schema is a pattern specified in general terms, and elaborated by instances in detailed ways. It emerges from entrenched instances or actual instances of language use. It serves as a template for describing existing units or creating new ones.

- The universal grammar-based model separates grammar from language use, or language function from language structure. Language acquisition emerges from a combination of rules which generate grammatical sentences. Frequency is irrelevant for the innate core of grammatical knowledge. In contrast, the usage-based model recognizes the influence of frequency on linguistic structure and language development. Linguistic structures and grammatical patterns that are frequently used in discourse become entrenched. Frequency aids in the storage of items in memory and affects the productivity of schemas by extending them to novel expressions.

- The universal grammar-based model focuses on the properties of the human mind, rather than on observable manifestations. It relates language to the intuitive knowledge of speakers, or inborn mental capacity. In contrast, the usage-based model is experience-driven, with knowledge of grammar grounded in experience. Knowledge of language exists through early experience with the language. Linguistic patterns as grounded in perceptual experience. Grammar reflects generalizations about phenomena in the world as speakers experience them. In this case, the actual sentences used to describe the world are the basis for devising the rules.

- In the universal grammar-based model, phenomena related to figurative language such as metaphor, metonymy and blending are seen as a kind of linguistic embellishment, or as decoration to ordinary language. In contrast, the usage-based model considers them textual manifestations of the workings of the human mind. They are linguistic manifestations of cognitive processes. The emergence of linguistic structure is crucially influenced by them. They are brought into play for the creation of novel ideas. They are fundamental components of the thought process, part of everyday discourse. They serve to signal emphasis, clarity and importance.

GLOSSARY

affective The speaker's feelings towards an expression, which differs from one person to another.
agent The entity that performs the action expressed by the verb.
ambiguity A phenomenon where an expression has multiple meanings, causing confusion.
anomaly The lexical relation where a lexical item does not fit the context it is used in.
anti-antonyms Pairs of lexical items that mean the same thing but appear opposite.
antonymy The lexical relation between two lexical items where one is the opposite of the other.
atomism The assumption that the meaning of a lexical item can be determined in isolation by its components.
attributive adjective An adjective that directly precedes the noun it describes.
auto-antonyms Pairs of lexical items that are homographs and mean opposite things.
backgrounding The act of giving less attention and importance to a part of a sentence.
base The domain relative to which the profile or figure is understood. Also known as **ground**.
blended space A created space resulting from the interaction of input spaces, with emergent meaning not found in either input. Also known as **blend**.
blending The mental operation that combines fragments of two lexical items to create a new complex lexical item. Also known as **conceptual integration**.
benefactive The entity that benefits from an action.
bottom-up General patterns emerging from specific ones.
categorization The mental act of grouping together the multiple senses of a linguistic item into a category. In the cognitive approach to language, categorization is based on prototypes.
category A network of distinct but related senses of a given linguistic item. The senses gather around a prototype, are defined by their resemblance to it and are arranged in terms of distance from it.
causer The thing that makes something happen.
classical The theory of linguistic meaning where humans categorize concepts by means of necessary and sufficient conditions. Also called check-list.
Cognitive Lexical Semantics An approach to lexical meaning that focuses on the cognitive aspects of language. It studies how language relates to meaning and cognition.
Cognitive Linguistics The general approach to language study that characterizes language as non-modular, symbolic, usage based, meaningful and creative.
cognitive processes Operations that reflect the capabilities of the mind or functions of the brain

in producing and interpreting linguistic expressions.

Cognitive Semantics The specific approach to linguistic meaning that characterizes linguistic meaning as embodied, motivated, dynamic, encyclopaedic and conceptualized.

co-hyponyms The set of lexical items that share the same superordinate term.

colligation A grammatical pattern which shows the position of a lexical item in a sentence and/or delimits the types of its complements.

collocability The ability of lexical items to combine with other items in a grammatically correct way.

collocation The habitual pairing of lexical items in a language. The case when two or more lexical items go together and form a common expression.

co-meronyms Lexical items which name the parts of the same whole.

compatibility The tendency of lexical items to co-occur in certain positions due to sharing specific syntactic and semantic features.

complex word A word that is composed of two or more substructures, which is morphologically divisible. Also called composite or polymorphemic.

Componential Analysis A type of definitional analysis in which the meaning of an expression is decomposed into a finite set of semantic components.

compound A blend formed by integrating two substructures, or a composite structure made up of two, or more, lexical items.

concept A mental representation realized in language by means of symbolic structures. It is the abstract meaning that a linguistic expression represents.

conceptual The meaning of an expression based on a mental concept in the speaker's mind.

conceptual content The property inherent in a situation, conventionally associated with an expression.

conceptualization The mental act of construing and expressing a situation in alternate ways.

conceptual mapping The mental operation that establishes correspondence between two conceptual domains, where an element in the first corresponds to its counterpart in the second.

Conceptual Semantics An approach to lexical meaning that breaks lexical concepts up into semantic categories, helping a person understand lexical items and provide an explanatory semantic representation.

conceptual structure The concept in the conceptual system that stands for the thing experienced, assembled for meaning construction purposes.

conceptual system Our knowledge of the world, the repository of the concepts available to a human being.

configuration The mental act of grouping together a number of linguistic items, be they lexical or grammatical, into a cognitive domain. The linguistic items share the same conceptual area but differ in specifics.

connotation The figural, cultural or emotional meaning associated with an expression.

connotative The additional meaning that a lexical item has beyond its denotative meaning.

construal The mental ability of a speaker to describe a situation in alternate ways and express them using different linguistic items. The **construal** theory considers meaning subjective.

context The physical environment in which a linguistic expression is used, referring to the location where the discussion takes place.

contextual meaning The meaning a linguistic expression has in a context.

conventional The literal meaning of an expression, the basic, original or usual meaning.

converse antonyms The relation between two lexical items where the existence of one implies the existence of the other.

contradictory A relationship between two expressions that are mutually opposed or inconsistent.

contrary A relationship between two expressions that are opposite in nature, direction or meaning.

decompositional The analysis of an expression in terms of semantic components.

denotation The literal, constant and basic meaning of an expression. It is the relationship between an expression and the kind of thing it refers to in the world. It is the core meaning that an expression has, as described in a dictionary.

denotative The literal meaning of a lexical item.

descriptive The meaning of a lexical item that bears on reference and truth. It includes the act of both referring to something and stating its truth.

diachronic lexicology The study of the evolution of lexical items and word-formation over time. Also called **historical lexicology**.

dictionary theory The theory according to which the core meaning of a linguistic item is the information contained in the item's definition. It focuses on linguistic knowledge in defining lexical items.

dictionary view A linguistic view in which a lexical concept represents a neatly packaged bundle of meaning that is given in a dictionary.

dynamic The meaning of a linguistic expression is flexible in the sense of extending its scope to express new experiences.

dysphemism The use of a derogatory or unpleasant term instead of a pleasant or neutral one.

embodied The structure of reality, as reflected in language, is a product of the human mind and human embodiment. The meaning of a linguistic expression is determined in large measure by the nature of our bodies.

encyclopaedic view A linguistic view in which a lexical concept serves as access sites to vast repositories of knowledge.

encyclopaedic theory The theory according to which the meaning of a linguistic item includes everything that is known about its referent. It focuses on both linguistic and non-linguistic knowledge in defining lexical items.

euphemism The phenomenon in which a lexical item or phrase is used instead of another to avoid being unpleasant, indecent or offensive.

experiencer The entity that is psychologically affected by an action.

expression The meaningful unit of language such as an affix, word, phrase or sentence.

expressive meaning The semantic quality of a linguistic expression, independent of the context in which it is used.

extension The extension of a lexical item is the set of referents it properly applies to.

extra-linguistic context Anything in the world outside of language that affects the interpretation of a lexical item.

figurative Language in which lexical items or phrases are meaningful, but not literally true. It is used to convey a complicated meaning, colourful writing, or evocative comparison.

figure The entity that is distinguished from a background, i.e. the **ground**.

focus The central point of a sentence in which speakers are most interested and to which they pay a special attention.

focusing The mental act of giving attention to one particular part of an expression rather than another.

foregrounding The act of highlighting a part of a sentence by making it the main point of attention and consequently emphasizing its importance. Also known as **highlighting**.

form The orthographic representation associated with a linguistic expression. The form serves to express meaning.

formalist The paradigm that focuses on the formal aspects of language. It includes the decompositional conceptions of meaning: componential, conceptual and primitive. It considers language a system which should be studied in isolation, from both its users and its cognitive processes.

frame The knowledge background with respect to which the meanings of lexical items can be properly described.

Frame semantics A theory of meaning according to which lexical meanings can only be properly understood and described against the background of a particular body of knowledge known as a **frame**.

Generative Lexical Semantics An approach to lexical meaning that breaks down meaning into smaller units called semantic components, or reduces meaning to a very restricted set of universal semantic primitives, or represent items as conceptual elements in the mind of an individual language use.

goal The entity towards which something moves.

gradable antonyms The lexical relation between two lexical items in which the degree of opposition is not absolute. Gradable antonyms normally have a **contrary** relation.

grammatical meaning The meaning that is conveyed in a sentence by the semantic roles and word order of its lexical items.

ground The background against which the figure stands out.

holism The thesis that what a linguistic expression means depends on its relations to many or all other expressions within the same totality.

holistic The assumption that the meaning of a lexical item is determined by its relations with the other items in the language.

holonym A lexical item which names the whole and includes parts.

homography The relation between two or more lexical items which are spelt alike but have different meanings and different pronunciations.

homonymy The relation between two lexical items which sound alike but differ in meaning, or the relation between two lexical items which have the same spelling but different meaning.

homophony The relation between two or more lexical items which are pronounced alike but have different spellings and meanings.

hypernym The superordinate lexical item which has a general meaning.

hyponym The subordinate lexical item which has a specific meaning.

hyponymy The lexical relation between two lexical items in which the meaning of one is included in the meaning of the other.

idiom A non-compositional expression that has a particular meaning that is different from the meanings of the individual items in it.

idiomaticity The lexical relation that deals with a group of lexical items whose meaning is different from the meanings of the individual items.

immediate scope The portion in an expression which is directly relevant for a particular purpose.

indeterminacy The difficulty of identifying the referent in an expression.

input spaces The spaces that represent relevant aspects of the concepts being combined. They correspond to the source and target domains of conceptual metaphor.

instrument The means by which something is done.

integration The mental operation that merges fragments of two lexical items to create a new complex lexical item. Also called blending.

intension The property or properties that allow the extension of a lexical item to be determined.

interspeaker variation The variation between languages. The variation between lexical items is constrained by the cultural context in which they occur.

intraspeaker variation The variation within the language. The variation between lexical items is constrained by the linguistic context in which they occur.

juxtaposition The ability of lexical items to combine horizontally.

language A structured inventory of linguistic units defined as form-meaning pairings used for communicating ideas and feelings.

language user A member of a particular linguistic community who uses language for the sake of communication.

lexical field The theory according to which the meaning of a linguistic item is described relative to the relationship it holds with its counterparts.

lexical hierarchy A systematic way of classifying lexical items by arranging them into categories. Also called **Taxonomy**.

lexical item A single item that forms the basic elements of a language's lexicon.

lexical meaning The literal meaning of a lexical item taken out of context, which is distinguished from its grammatical meaning.

lexical relationship The connection that is established between one lexical item and another.

Lexical Semantics The branch of semantics which deals with the meanings of lexical items.

lexicology The branch of linguistics that analyses the lexicon of a specific language.

lexicon The stock of lexical items that make up a language. Also known as **lexis**.

linguistic context The set of lexical items that occur immediately before and/or after a lexical item in a phrase or sentence.

linguistics The scientific study of language. It studies the cognitive processes involved in producing and understanding language.

literal meaning The meaning of a lexical item taken out of context.

location The place where an action happens.

matrix The set of domains which provides the context for the full understanding of a semantic unit.

maximalist An approach that addresses all of language, not just certain levels of representation.

maximal scope The full extent of the coverage of an expression.

meaning The semantic content associated with a linguistic expression. The meaning is expressed by form.

meaningful The claim that all language elements have semantic values. Language is a means of conveying meaning; therefore all its resources serve to carry out this function.

meronym The lexical item which names the part of another item.

meronymy The lexical relation between two lexical items in which the meaning of one names a part of the meaning of the other. Also known as **partonymy**.

metaphor The form of conceptual structure that involves mapping between two things from distinct areas of knowledge, where one is compared with the other.

metonymy The form of conceptual structure that involves mapping between two things within the same area of knowledge, where the name of one is substituted for the name of the other with which it is connected in some respect.

monosemy The association of one lexical item with one meaning.

morphology A branch of linguistics which studies the structure of words. It analyses how prefixes and suffixes are added to form words.

motivated The relationship between the form and meaning of a linguistic expression is often motivated or inseparable. The meaning of a linguistic expression arises as the outcome of stimulation to achieve a desired goal.

maximal scope The view in which the speaker considers a broad range of content in describing a situation.

narrow view The perspective in which the speaker considers a limited range of content in describing a situation.

Natural Semantic Metalanguage An approach to linguistic meaning in which the meaning of an expression can be defined in terms of a small set of semantic primes or primitives.

non-figurative Literal language that conveys exactly and directly what it means, without figures of speech such as metaphors or metonymies.

non-gradable antonyms The lexical relation between two lexical items in which the degree of opposition is absolute. Non-gradable antonyms typically have a **contradictory** relation. Also known as **complementaries** or **binary antonyms**.

non-modular An approach to language that argues there is no autonomous portion of the brain which is specialized for language. Linguistic abilities are inseparable from other cognitive abilities.

non-reductionist An approach that lists highly specific patterns as well as more general patterns.

non-reversible lexical pair A pair of items used together in a stable order which is logically consistent.

objectivism The theory that symbols used in language derive from their meaning via correspondence with things in the external world.

objectivist The theory of meaning that views meaning in terms of the correlation between what is said and what is seen.

objectivity The dimension in which the speaker expresses distance from the situation being described, excluding the self from the scene described.

pairing The act of matching the phonological and semantic poles of a linguistic expression for communicative purposes.

paradigmatic relationship A pattern of relationship between lexical items in a vertical order, based on the criterion of **substitution**.

partonymy The relation between two lexical items in which the meaning of one names a part of the meaning of the other.

patient The entity that undergoes the action expressed by the verb.

periphery The remaining members in a category that contain some, but not all, of the attributes.

perspective The specific way of viewing a situation, which can change based on one's intention.

phonetics A branch of linguistics that studies how speech sounds are produced in a language.

phonology A branch of linguistics that studies how speech sounds function in a language.

pleonasm The use of a lexical item to emphasize what is already clear without it.

polyseme A lexical item or phrase that has multiple meanings.

polysemy The tendency of a linguistic item, whether lexical or grammatical, to have a range of different meanings that are related in some way.

possessor The entity that owns something or has a particular quality at one's disposal.

pragmatics A branch of linguistics that studies the meanings of lexical items, phrases and sentences in context.

predicative adjective An adjective that follows a linking verb and modifies the subject of the linking verb.

prescriptivism An approach to language that emphasizes enforcing rules on how language should be used.

primitives Indivisible atoms of meaning that combine to form a more complex meaning.

profile The conceptual referent within the array of conceptual content invoked by the item. Also known as figure.

profiling The mental act of singling out a substructure that functions as the focal point of attention in an expression.

prominence The quality of eminence given, often in varying degrees, to the substructures of a conception relative to their importance.

proposition The semantic content of an expression that describes a state of affairs in the world.

prototype The ideal or central member of a category that assembles the key attributes of the category.

reference The theory of meaning in which the meaning of a lexical item is tied to an actual object in the world.

referent The specific entity for which an expression stands on any occasion of use.

referential The meaning of an expression that derives from its reference to an actual object in the external world.

relational The concept that the meaning of an expression is determined by its position in a network in which it is related to other expressions.

relational antonyms The lexical relation between two lexical items that are not susceptible to degrees of opposition, and are not an either-or matter in character.

representational The concept that the meaning of an expression is linked to a particular mental representation, termed a **concept**.

reversive antonyms The relation between two lexical items that involves opposition in direction.

reversible lexical pair A pair of items used together capable of switching with concomitant meaning differences.

schematicity A coarse-grained description of an expression. It involves minimum attention to detail.

scope The array of conceptual content that an expression specifically evokes and relies upon for its characterization.

selection restrictions Syntactic-semantic restrictions that govern the co-occurrence of lexical items.

semantic components The features of meaning that combine to form a complex meaning. Also known as **semantic features**.

semantic primes Indivisible atoms of meaning that combine to form a more complex meaning. Also known as **primitives**.

semantic prosody The pattern in which a lexical item co-occurs with other items belonging to a particular semantic set.

semantic roles The semantic relations that link a verb to its arguments. Also known as **functional/thematic/participant**.

semantics A branch of linguistic that studies the meanings of lexical items, phrases and sentences.

semantic structure The meaning that stands for the conceptual structure, conventionally associated with linguistic expressions.

sense The concept represented by the meaning of an expression, basic to its individual identity.

sense relation A pattern of association that exists between lexical items in a language, including paradigmatic and syntagmatic relations.

simple word A word composed of only one lexical structure, morphologically indivisible. Also known as **monomorphemic**.

social The meaning of a lexical item governed by the social rules of interaction, indicating the social relationship between the speaker and the addressee.

source (i) The entity from which something moves. (ii) In metaphor, aspects of a more familiar area of knowledge are compared with aspects of a less familiar area of knowledge called the **target**.

specificity A fine-grained description of an expression, involving maximum attention to detail.

Structural Lexical Semantics An approach to lexical meaning in which the meaning of a lexical item derives from its relation to other lexical items in the language. Also known as **relational** approach.

structured The property of units being related to one another in organized ways.

subjectivism The theory that symbols used in language derive their meaning from correspondence with conceptualizations of the world. Also known as **experientialism**.

subjectivist The theory of meaning that emphasizes the importance of world experience in the representation of linguistic expressions and recognizes the speaker's capacity to construe a situation in alternative ways.

subjectivity The dimension in which the speaker expresses involvement in the situation being described, representing a close relationship between the speaker and the content of the situation.

subordinate The meaning of a lexical item that display a high degree of specificity.

substance The form and meaning of an expression has, with form being the phonological representation and meaning the idea conventionally associated with it.

substitution The ability of lexical items to replace each other vertically within a particular context.

superordinate The meaning of a lexical item that displays a high degree of generality.

symbolic The claim that language is a set of symbols or conventional means available to language users for representing ideas or communicating thought.

synchronic/modern lexicology The study of the vocabulary of a language at any given point in time, usually the present.

synonymy The lexical relation between two lexical items in which the meaning of one is similar, but not identical, to the meaning of the other.

synonym A lexical item that has the same or nearly the same meaning as another in the same language.

syntagmatic relation The pattern of relation between lexical items in a linear order, based on the criterion of **juxtaposition**.

syntax A branch of linguistics that studies the structure of sentences.

target In metaphor, aspects of a less familiar area of knowledge are compared with aspects of a more familiar area of knowledge, called the **source**.

taxonomy The systematic classification of lexical items by arranging them into categories. Also known as **lexical hierarchy**.

theme The neutral role; the entity is neither acting itself nor being acted on by an agent.

time The time when an action happens.

Traditional Lexical Semantics An approach to lexical meaning in which the meaning of lexical item resides in the linkage between its meaning and the object in the real world, or is reducible to, its truth conditions.

truth conditions The conditions of objective external reality against which an expression can be judged true or false.

truth-conditional The theory that sees the meaning of an expression as being the same as, or reducible to, its truth conditions.

unconventional The non-literal meaning of an expression that goes beyond the dictionary meaning.

usage Usage refers to the way a lexical item is commonly used in language.

use Use refers to the act of employing a lexical item for its intended purpose.

usage based The quality of linguistic units being authentic, with language patterns emerging from generalizations made from actual instances of language use.

usage event A specific utterance of language use, employed to convey a particular meaning.

utterance An actual instance of language use.

vagueness Lack of referential clarity, resulting from providing little information about something.

vantage point The position from which the same objective situation is observed and described, resulting in different construals and different structures.

word A symbolic unit with an identifiable meaning and a phonological shape, a combination of meaning and form.

word order The order of syntactic constituents within phrases, clauses or sentences. Also known as **linear order**.

zeugma The use of a lexical item that must be interpreted in two different ways simultaneously to make sense.

ANSWER KEY

Part I

Chapter 1

Practice 1.1
1. c   2. d   3. a   4. e   5. b

Practice 1.2
1. un<u>likely</u>   2. en<u>ligh</u>ten   3. <u>trus</u>teeship   4. <u>grue</u>somely   5. dis<u>agree</u>able

Practice 1.3
1. lexical knowledge   2. Encyclopaedic knowledge   3. polysemy
4. frames   5. construal

Practice 1.4
1. bank — financial institution/margin of a river.
2. backward — a place that is behind/less developed
3. court — a place for justice administration/an open space enclosed wholly or partly by buildings.
4. glasses — spectacles/drinking vessels
5. record — the top performance in sport/a disc on which music is stored.

Chapter 2

Practice 2.1
This is a sample list of meanings.

1. She stretched her arms out. (upper limb)
   It is not easy to escape the arm of the law. (power)
   The research arm of the government. (branch)
2. She has a dinner date. (appointment)
   The date is delicious. (the fruit of date palm)
   Childhood has so short a date. (duration)
3. I a drop of blue ink. (liquid)
   It's only a four-foot drop. (vertical distance)
   There is a drop in prices. (a decrease in value)

4. Patricia looked elegant as always. (stylish)
   She gave an elegant solution to the problem. (simple)
   That is an absolutely elegant wine. (excellent)
5. Slowly, I turned the door handle. (to move in a circle)
   Turn right at the traffic lights. (to change direction)
   The weather has suddenly turned cold. (to become)

Practice 2.2
1. A tennis player is a person who plays tennis.
2. A guitar player is a person who plays the guitar.
3. A stage player is a person who acts on the stage.
4. A market player is a person who is involved in buying and selling.
5. A card player is a person who plays card games.

Practice 2.3
1. *Throw* means causing an object to move rapidly through the air, as in *The kids were outside throwing snowballs at each other*. *Hurl* means throwing an object forcefully or violently, as in *In a fit of temper he hurled the book across the room*.

2. *Thrifty* means being careful about spending money and not wasting things. Thrifty is characterized by economy and good management. *He is thrifty and never gets into debt*. *Stingy* means sparing or scant in using, giving or spending money. *He's stingy and never buys anyone a drink when we go out*.

3. *Bargain* means disputing softly or normally over the price of something, as in *He bargained with the taxi driver over the fare*. *Haggle* means arguing harshly, heatedly or noisily over the price of something, as in *They spent hours haggling over prices*.

4. *Unique* means being the only one of its kind; unequalled, unparalleled or unmatched, as in *Everyone's fingerprints are unique*. *Peculiar* means strange, odd, unusual or out of the ordinary, as in *The man has a rather peculiar sense of humour*.

5. *Easygoing* describes a person as being calm, relaxed or casual, as in *He was easygoing and good-natured*. *Lackadaisical* describes a person as showing no interest or enthusiasm in what he does, as in *My neighbour seemed a little lackadaisical at times*.

Practice 2.4
1. *Kidnap* is used when a person has been taken away by force. *Hijack* is used when a vehicle is taken over by force.

2. *Heal* refers to the ongoing process of becoming well. *Cure* refers to the complete elimination of a disease.

3. A *habit* is something that a person does often or regularly, usually as a result of personal preference. A *custom* is something that people in a society do at a particular time of year or in a particular situation, usually as a result of cultural or historical tradition.

4. A *trip* usually refers to travelling to a place and returning back to where one started. A *journey* refers to travelling from one place to another, but not necessarily returning to where one started.

5. A *problem* is a specific difficulty that has to be resolved or dealt with. It is connected to solutions. *Trouble* is a general difficulty that causes negative feelings, distress or worry. It is less connected to solutions.

Practice 2.5
1. The interjection *ah* expresses surprise.
2. The interjection *alas* expresses distress.
3. The interjection *hey* expresses indifference.
4. The interjection *ugh* expresses disgust.
5. The interjection *wow* expresses admiration.

Practice 2.6
1. tomboy vs. sissy   gender
Tomboy and *sissy* are used to describe individuals who may not conform to traditional gender expectations. *Tomboy* is often associated with girls who display more masculine characteristics, while *sissy* is used to describe boys who exhibit more feminine traits, reflecting underlying societal expectations and stereotypes.

2. youthful vs. elderly   age
Youthful evokes attributes such as vitality, vigour, optimism, innovation and socializing. Elderly evokes attributes such as maturity, wisdom, experience and frailty.

3. blue-collar vs. white-collar   class
Blue-collar is associated with manual labour and trade occupations, while *white-collar* is often associated with professional and managerial roles, reflecting class-based distinctions within the workforce.

4. macho vs. effeminate   gender
Macho often conveys exaggerated masculinity, while *effeminate* may suggest that a man's behaviour or appearance aligns more closely with traditional feminine traits, often carrying social judgements and implications.

5. *Poverty* may evoke notions of struggle, lack of opportunity and systemic disadvantage, while *affluence* is associated with abundance, privilege and social influence, reflecting class-based inequalities and perceptions.

Practice 2.7
1. indisposed   2. slim   3. economical   4. disabled   5. curious

Chapter 3

Practice 3.1
1. time   2. agent   3. benefactive   4. location   5. instrument
6. experiencer   7. patient   8. source   9. causer   10. theme

Practice 3.2
In the sentences, the lexical item *only* is used in five different positions. In each, the meaning is different. The first sentence means that only I asked him a question, no

one else. The second sentence means that I only asked him a question, not answer. The third sentence means that I asked only him a question, no one else. The fourth means that I asked him only a question, nothing else. The fifth sentence means that I asked him a question only about history, not geography.

Practice 3.3
1. a. a private house offering accommodation to paying guests.
   b. a guest entertained in one's house.
2. a. paper for covering walls of rooms.
   b. a wall made of paper.
3. a. a shoe made of leather.
   b. leather used to make shoes.
4. a. a garden featuring flowering plants.
   b. a flower that grows in a garden.
5. a. a boat which is filled for use as a dwelling.
   b. a building where boats are stored.

Practice 3.4
1. saucer   2. forth   3. alive   4. sound   5. thread

Part II

Chapter 4

Practice 4.1
1. *Interfere* has a negative connotation. It means meddling in something that is not one's concern.
   Intervene has a more positive connotation. It means to get involved in a conflict situation to prevent it from getting worse.

2. *Clever* connotes being creative, skilful or adept. It means dexterous at making things by hand.
   Intelligent connotes intellectual capacity. It means mentally capable.

3. *Alone* connotes a state of isolation when one is outside the company of others.
   Lonely connotes a feeling of sadness when one is abandoned.

4. *Beautiful* connotes a deeper level of attractiveness.
   Pretty connotes a more superficial level of attractiveness.

5. *Upset* connotes a sadder, gentler emotion. When one is upset, one may want to cry or curl up in bed until one feels better.
   Angry connotes a stronger, more aggressive emotion. When one is angry, one might want to yell, fight or throw something.

Practice 4.2
1. Non-referring/Referring
2. Referring/Non-referring
3. Non-referring/Referring

4. Non-referring/Referring
5. Referring/Non-Referring

Practice 4.3

1. *Ache* is discomfort that continues for some time. It is usually associated with a specific part of the body, such as a headache, a stomach ache, a toothache or an earache. It is usually not extremely strong, so you can try to ignore it.
Pain is a sharp, localized sensation. It arises when one cuts oneself or hits the head on something. It is usually stronger, more sudden and more difficult to ignore.

2. A *hotel* offers private rooms with private facilities. Hotels are luxurious, but they tend to be less social.
A *hostel* offers dorm rooms, with shared facilities. Hostels have a community feel, but they offer less privacy.

3. *Salary* is the fixed amount of compensation which is paid for the performance of an employee.
Wage is the variable amount of compensation which is paid on an hourly basis for finishing a certain amount of work.

4. *Award* is always given by someone for achieving something exceptional. It is given publically through a systematic process. An award can be a trophy, medal, prize or certificate.
Reward is a recognition or acknowledgement for one's efforts, contribution or service. It is given privately without a systematic process. A reward can be money or a word of praise.

5. *Holiday* refers to a short period that one spends doing leisure activities.
Vacation refers to a long period of time that one takes off from school or work.

Chapter 5

Practice 5.1

1. *Frail* implies delicacy and slightness of structure, as in *The teenager is too frail to enjoy sports.*

2. *Weak* applies to deficiency or inferiority in strength or power of any sort, as in *She felt weak after the surgery.*

3. *Feeble* suggests extreme weakness inviting pity or contempt, as in *She made a feeble attempt to walk.*

4. *Fragile* suggests frailty, brittleness and inability to resist rough usage, as in *The reclusive poet is too fragile for the rigors of this world.*

5. *Decrepit* implies being worn out or broken down from long use or old age, as in *A decrepit elderly man sat on a park bench.*

Practice 5.2
1. reversive
2. gradable
3. relational

4. non-gradable
5. converse

Practice 5.3
1. clip	attach, or cut off
2. dust	remove dust (cleaning a house), or add dust (e.g., dust a cake with sugar).
3. ravel	separate (e.g., threads in cloth), or entangle.
4. cleave	cling, or to split apart.
5. sanction	approve, or penalize.

Practice 5.4
1. run
   1. to go faster than walking, as in *I had to run to catch the bus.*
   2. to go in a particular direction, as in *The road runs along the side of a lake.*
   3. to be in charge of something, as in *They run a restaurant in Leeds.*
2. foot
   1. the lowest part of the leg, as in *What size foot have you got?*
   2. the bottom of something, as in *There is a note at the foot of the page.*
   3. a measure of length, as in *She is five feet two inches tall.*
3. over
   1. above or more, as in *Children of 14 and over are invited to the programme.*
   2. across a street, as in *I stopped and crossed over.*
   3. remaining, not used, as in *If there's any food left over, put it in the fridge.*
4. plain
   1. simple in style, as in *The rooms are quite plain.*
   2. honest, as in *I will be plain with you.*
   3. clear, as in *The instructions were very plain.*
5. mouth
   1. Body part, as in *Don't talk with your mouth full.*
   2. a person in need of food, as in *They cannot support all the hungry mouths.*
   3. the opening of something, as in *They took a picture near the mouth of the cave.*

Practice 5.5
No two lexical items have the same meaning. Apply this tenet to the following pairs and show how different they are in meaning.

1. wet = moist
2. soft = tender
3. coarse = rough
4. strong = robust
5. tremble = shiver

Practice 5.6
1. grilling, roasting, frying
2. dogs, elephants, dolphins
3. knives, forks, spoons
4. trains, cars, planes
5. cups, plates, bowls

Practice 5.7
1. wheel, engine, tire
2. ceiling, door, window
3. cellar, kitchen, study
4. flash, lens, tripod
5. monitor, keyboard, mouse

Practice 5.8
1. I heard a lion roaring.
2. The plant died.
3. The engine needs petrol.
4. The woman drank water.
5. Mutton is meat from sheep.

Practice 5.9
1. verb + noun	break promise	pay attention	save energy
2. noun + noun	air raid	car park	office hours
3. verb + adverb	speak loudly	regret deeply	agree strongly
4. adjective + noun	quick meal	fast food	heavy rain
5. adverb + adjective	completely sure	slightly late	ridiculously easy
6. noun + verb	dogs bark	cats purr	lions roar
7. verb + preposition	run out of time	swell with pride	burst into tears

Practice 5.10
Some lexical items combine with multiple prepositions. When one preposition is replaced with another, the meaning is completely altered. How?

1. agree on something	agree with someone
2. arrive at a building	arrive in a city/country
3. ask about someone	ask for something
4. happy for someone	happy about something
5. angry at something	angry with someone
6. think of (a past event)	think about (considering an idea)
7. blame for something	blame on someone
8. throw at (hurl someone/something)	throw to (aim for someone/something)
9. impact of something as agent	impact on something as patient
10. responsible for someone/something as agent	responsible to someone/something as patient

Practice 5.11
1. like   + -ing gerund/to-infinitive, as in *I like swimming/to swim.*
2. make   + bare infinitive, as in *She always makes me laugh.*
3. recall + -ing gerund, as in *I can't recall meeting her before.*
4. intend + -ing gerund/to-infinitive, as in *I intend staying/to stay long.*
5. pledge + to-infinitive, as in *They pledged to continue campaigning.*

Practice 5.12

1. sit tight	wait patiently and take no action
2. hit the hay	want to go to sleep
3. give a shot	give it a try
4. cut corners	reduce time, money and expenses
5. break the ice	become friends with
6. keep an eye on	watch or look after something or someone
7. draw a longbow	lie
8. make ends meet	manage expenses
9. pull someone's leg	trick someone
10. keep your chin up	be brave

Chapter 6

Practice 6.1

1. juror	a member of a jury who decides the verdict in a trial.
2. referee	an official who controls the game in certain sports.
3. reviewer	a person who writes reviews of books, films or plays.
4. surveyor	a person who measures and records the details of a piece of land.
5. arbitrator	a person who is chosen to settle a disagreement.

Practice 6.2

1. bag	a container made of cloth, plastic or leather, used for carrying shopping or travelling items.
2. box	a container made of wood, cardboard or metal, used for holding books, tools or matches.
3. sack	a container made of strong paper or plastic, used for storing flour or coal.
4. packet	a small container made of paper or cardboard used for packing biscuits, cigarettes or crisps.
5. wallet	a small container made of leather or plastic used for keeping paper money or credit cards in.

Practice 6.3

1. shun	avoid something as a matter of habitual practice or policy. It may imply repugnance or abhorrence, as in *She has shunned publicity since she retired from the theatre.*
2. avoid	stress forethought and caution in keeping clear of danger or difficulty, as in *They built a wall to avoid soil being washed away.*
3. evade	implies adroitness, ingenuity or lack of scruple in avoiding something, as in *He evaded the question by changing the subject.*
4. escape	stresses the fact of getting away or being passed by not necessarily through effort or by conscious intent, as in *She was lucky to escape serious injury.*
5. eschew	implies deliberately avoiding or keeping away from something as unwise or distasteful, as in *We won't have discussions with this group unless they eschew violence.*

# Part III

Chapter 7

Practice 7.1
1. boat   row boat, sailboat, motor boat, fishing boat, paddle boat
2. food   vegetables, fruits, dairy products, meat and poultry, cereals
3. sports   team sports (football, basketball, baseball), individual sports (tennis, golf, swimming), racquet sports (badminton, squash, table tennis), water sports (surfing, sailing, diving), Winter sports (skiing, snowboarding, ice skating)
4. hobbies   collecting, gardening, reading, puzzles, sports
5. clothing   business attire, casual wear, formal wear, lingerie, sportswear

Practice 7.2
A chair is a seat for one person that has a back and four legs. A kitchen chair is regarded as the prototype of the chair category because it possesses almost all the features. The remaining examples are ranked as follows relative to their closeness to the prototype: armchair, rocking chair, swivel chair, wheelchair and highchair.

Practice 7.3
The verb drive is polysemous. Prototypically, it has the following senses. (a) 'to make a vehicle move along'. In this sense, the agent is human, while the thing driven is a concrete entity, as in *She drives a red sports car*. (b) 'to take someone somewhere in a car'. In this sense, the thing driven is a concrete human entity, as in *She drove Anna to London*. (c) 'to force something into a state'. In this sense, the thing driven is an abstract entity, as in *The government has driven the economy into deep recession*. (d) 'to force someone to go somewhere'. In this sense, both the agent and the thing driven are human, as in *They drove the occupying troops from the city*. (e) 'a short private road which leads from a public road to a house', as in *I parked in the drive*. (f) 'a journey in a car', as in *Shall we go for a drive this afternoon*?

    Peripherally, the verb drive has the following senses. (a) 'to provide the power to keep something working'. In this sense, both the agent and the thing driven are concrete non-human entities, as in *The engine drives the wheels*. (b) 'to force someone into a particular state, often an unpleasant one';. In this sense, the agent is an abstract entity, whereas the thing driven is a concrete human entity, as in *Love has driven men and women to strange extremes*. (c) 'to force someone into a particular state, often an unpleasant one'. In this sense, both the agent and the thing driven are concrete human entities, as in *She's driving me crazy*. (d) 'energy and determination to achieve things', as in *We are looking for someone with drive and ambition*. (e) 'a planned effort to achieve something', as in *The latest promotional material is all part of a recruitment drive*. (f) 'to state something in a very forceful and effective way', as in *The speaker really drove his message home, repeating his main point several times*.

Chapter 8

Practice 8.1
1. *Hire* means to employ somebody for a short time to do a particular job, as in *They hired a firm of consultants to design the new system.*

2. *Employ* means to give somebody a job to do for payment, as in *The company employs 1200 people.*

3. *Engage* means to employ somebody to do a particular job, as in *He is currently engaged as a consultant.*

4. *Recruit* means to find new people to join a company, an organization or the armed forces, as in *They recruited several new members to the club.*

5. *Appoint* means to choose somebody for a job or position of responsibility, as in *They have appointed him (as) captain of the team.*

Practice 8.2
People split cost or prize, chop onions or carrots, crack paint or glass, carve wood or stone and divide money.

Practice 8.3
1. They were evicted from the flat for not paying their rent.
2. She was expelled from school for setting fire to the library.
3. He was banished from New Zealand for political reasons.
4. She was dismissed from the firm for calling her boss a liar.
5. He was discharged from the hospital after recovering from illness.

Chapter 9

Practice 9.1
1. The lexical item *work* is a more general term that does not specify the role. The lexical item *job* refers to a specific occupation or profession.

2. The lexical item *goal* is a general term, as in *Our goal is to improve health care for children.* The lexical item *objective* is a specific term, as in *Our objective is to provide 10,000 children with vaccines.*

3. The lexical item *illness* is general. It describes the condition of poor health, but it is not specific about what is causing the health problems. The lexical item *disease* is specific. It is used when the human body is not functioning correctly due to infection, genetic defects or other problems.

4. The lexical item *incident* refers to any event: big or small, good or bad, intentional or unintentional, as in a bank robbery. The lexical item *accident* is a bad event caused by error or by chance. Accidents are always unintentional, and they usually result in some damage or injury, as in a car crash.

5. The lexical item *guarantee* is a general term used for products and non-products. The lexical item *warranty* is a specific term used for products only.

Practice 9.2
1. Distance 2. Time 3. Degree 4. Progress 5. Difficulty 6. Wise
7. Effect 8. Very drunk or ill 9. Importance 10. Success.

Practice 9.3
1. The lexical item *coast* is used from the vantage point of someone coming from the land, as in *We drove for three hours until reaching the coast*. The lexical item *shore* is used from the vantage point of someone coming from the water, as in *The lighthouse helps boats reach the shore safely*.

2. The lexical item *borrow* means to take something from someone. It represents the vantage point of the receiver. The lexical item *lend* means to give something to someone. It represents the vantage point of the giver.

3. The lexical item *floor* is used for indoor surfaces. From the vantage point of someone inside the house, one can say *She dropped your bag on the floor*. The lexical item *ground* is used for outdoor surfaces. From the vantage point of someone outside the house, one can say *She dropped the bag on the ground*.

4. The lexical item *external* is simply what can be seen from outside, as in *an external staircase*; whereas the lexical item *exterior* suggests a judgement made from inside, as in *no exterior window*.

5. The lexical item *emigrate* means to leave one country or region to settle in another. The lexical item *immigrate* means to come to a country of which one is not a native, usually for permanent residence. The difference relates to the vantage point. In the first, the speaker is inside the country. In the second, the speaker is outside the country.

Practice 9.4
1. To assure someone is to remove someone's doubts. To assure someone of something means to convey the belief that whatever the person is worried or unsure about will happen, as in *My mother assured me that she would be present for the ceremony*. To ensure something is to make sure it happens, i.e. to guarantee it. *Ensure* means to perform all the necessary actions required to obtain the desired result, as in *She studied hard to ensure that she secures the first place in class*.

2. Both *accuse* and *charge* describe blaming someone for something. However, there is a difference in their usage. *Accuse* is to claim or assert that someone has done something wrong. It is used in any situation where someone is being blamed for something. It is based only on a belief, as in *He accused them of drinking beer while driving*. *Charge* is to formally do so, with the weight of the law behind you. It is used in the context of legal proceedings, where it refers to the formal accusation of a crime. It is based on credible evidence, as in *The police officer charged the suspect with vandalism*.

3. Both *adverse* and *averse* are used to indicate opposition. *Adverse* usually applies to things, effects or events. It conveys a sense of hostility or harmfulness, as in *Medicine has adverse effects*. *Averse* usually applies to people. It means feeling opposed or disinclined, as in *He is averse to taking risks*.

4. Both *delusion* and *illusion* refer to false perceptions. Although they seem interchangeable in some contexts, their implications are slightly different. *Delusion* suggests that the chronic false belief is subjective and results from distorted thinking within the individual, or a disordered mind, as in *He still lives under the delusion that he owns this place*. *Illusion* suggests that the temporary false belief is objective and results from external objects or circumstances, as in *Floor-to-ceiling windows can give the illusion of extra height*. In short, delusion is a mental phenomenon, whereas illusion is a physical phenomenon.

5. Both *certitude* and *certainty* imply an absence of doubt about the truth of something, however, they are distinguishable in use. *Certitude* is a subjective feeling of absolute conviction or belief in something, as in *We have the certitude that he will be freed*. *Certainty* is an objective feeling that involves inherent factuality. It refers to something that is established or verified. It is restricted to situations, results, information, etc., that can be shown objectively to be true, as in *Her return to the team now seems a certainty*.

Practice 9.5

1. Both *review* and *revise* play crucial roles in the writing process. They may seem interchangeable. Yet, there is a subtle difference between them. *Review* means just to look at a piece of written work or think about it. This means that you only read and carefully look at something again and again, as in *I need to review the chapter before the exam*. *Revise* means to edit a piece of written work, making changes and corrections. Unlike the verb review, revise includes changing or altering something to make it better, as in *He revised the letter because it was erroneous*.

2. Both *gather* and *collect* mean to bring things together, but there is a subtle difference in meaning between them. *Gather* has the sense of bringing together something in one place, as in *She gathered all the toys in the closet*. *Collect* refers to picking up things in sequence, i.e. keeping them close to each other, as in *She collects antique glass*.

3. Both *extend* and *expand* mean to make something bigger, but there is a difference in meaning. *Extend* means making something longer in one direction. It applies to things that are being stretched out, implying length, as in *Our land extends as far as the river*. *Expand* means making bigger in all directions. It applies to things that are spread out, implying area, as in *They have plans to expand the local airport*.

4. Both *specimen* and *sample* are used to refer to a portion or piece of a larger whole, but they have distinct applications. A *specimen* is an individual member of a sample, as in *Job applicants have to submit a specimen of handwriting*. A *sample* is a subset taken for some purpose from a larger population, as in *They asked the painter to present some sample drawings*.

5. Both *dilemma* and *quandary* are used for complicated and problematic situations, but there is a small difference between them. A *dilemma* is a situation in which a specific choice has to be made between two alternatives, especially ones that are equally undesirable, as in *She faces the dilemma of disobeying her father or losing the man she loves*. A *quandary* is a state of perplexity or uncertainty especially as requiring a choice between equally unfavourable options, as in *The government is in a quandary about what to do with so many people*.

Practice 9.6

1. Both *imply* and *infer* are often confused, but they have different focuses. *Imply* focuses on or suggests something indirectly, as in *Her remarks implied a threat*. *Infer* focuses on or guesses something based on what has been suggested, i.e. to derive a conclusion from facts or premises, as in *We see smoke and infer fire*.

2. Both *whole* and *entire* refer to complete things, but there is a difference in focus. *Whole* focuses on something as one complete package or a single entity, as in *I spent the whole day cleaning*. *Entire* focuses on all parts of something working independently, as in *I spent the entire month reading the book*.

3. Both *assume* and *presume* mean to take something for granted as true, but there is a difference in the degree of certainty. *Assume* is a guess based on little or no evidence, as in *I assume he'll be there*. *Presume* a guess based on reasonable evidence, as in *The missing journalist is presumed dead*.

4. Both *replace* and *substitute* refer to the use of one thing in place of another, but they are not interchangeable. *Replace* refers to a complete exchange of one thing for another, as in *Jets have largely replaced propeller planes*. *Substitute* involves using something else in place of the original item, as in *They substituted plastic for steel to reduce the weight*. In short, *replace* has a sense of permanence, whereas *substitute* has a sense of temporariness.

5. Both *bother* and *disturb* mean discomfort, but they differ in focus. *Bother* focuses on annoying someone, as in *The loud music from the party next door bothered me*. *Disturb* focuses on interfering with someone's peace of mind, as in *The noise from the construction site disturbed my concentration*. Of the two, *disturb* sounds more serious.

Chapter 10

Practice 10.1
1. Life is compared to a maze in having its navigation as one moves ahead with surprises at every turn.
2. Love is compared to a journey. It is a never-ending adventure. It has its ups and downs.
3. Her home is compared to a prison. She is trapped inside. She may be afraid of the outside.
4. The home is compared to a castle, where he can do whatever he wants. He is the ultimate ruler.
5. The area is compared to an anthill. It is buzzing with people.

Practice 10.2
1. Hurting feelings is like inflicting on someone with physical pain.
2. Swimming in emails is like being caught up in a sea of emails.
3. Temper flaring is like burning something. It means becoming angry.
4. Digging up information is like digging holes in an area of land.
5. Breaking into a conversation is like getting into a building by force.

Practice 10.3
1. Instead of starving for food, she is emotionally neglected and so starved for love.
2. He has a generous nature. Gold is something valued for its goodness.
3. A straight shooter is an honest and outspoken person. He is straightforward in dealings with others.
4. She expresses strong emotional feelings through a speech, story or help.
5. A budding relationship is a relationship that is still in its early stages. It is a romantic relationship that is just beginning and looks promising.

Chapter 11

Practice 11.1
1. The blade
2. British national press
3. Senior officers
4. Alcohol
5. President.

Practice 11.2
1. (i.e. object of glory) passion for object
2. (i.e. his novels). Author for works
3. Place for inhabitants
4. (i.e. sunshine, the effect is indicated by the sun, its cause). Cause for effect: attention is paid to the effect using its cause.
5. (i.e. old age, their cause) should be respected. Effect for cause: the effect is named to indicate its cause

Practice 11.3
1. The ear is a substitute for attention.
2. Sceptre is a substitute for power.
3. Tongue is a substitute for language.
4. Pen is a substitute for diplomacy. The sword is a substitute for violence.
5. The cradle is a substitute for birth, while the grave is a substitute for death.

Chapter 12

Practice 12.1
1. (global + English)
2. (television + photogenic)
3. (blizzard + disaster)
4. (box + exercise)
5. (sports + broadcast)

Practice 12.2
1. (video + blog)
2. (electronic + mail)
3. (biography + picture)

4. (romantic + comedy)
5. (friend + enemy)

Practice 12.3
1. (fan + magazine)
2. (mock + cocktail)
3. (stay + vacation)
4. (work + alcoholic)
5. (dumb + confound)

Chapter 13

Practice 13.1
1. enquire   2. reserve   3. verify   4. receive   5. request
6. assist   7. preserve   8. inform   9. permit   10. fight

Practice 13.2
The adjective *old* can be interpreted as meaning 'experienced' or 'outdated' depending on the context. In describing a goal, the adjective *lofty* can admirably imply the goal is respectable, or critically imply the goal is too ambitious to achieve. In some cultures, the adjective *polite* means using formal language and showing deference to authority figures, while in other cultures, being polite may mean being more informal and using humour to diffuse tense situations. In describing prices, the adjective *cheap* can be interpreted as meaning 'inexpensive' or 'of poor quality' depending on the context and cultural background of the speaker and listener. In describing a party, the adjective *extravagant* can mean critically profligate, i.e. spending too much or overly elaborate, or wonderfully abundant.

INDEX

A
affective 21, 182
agent 27, 182
ambiguity 7, 182
anomaly 64, 182
anti-antonyms 58–9, 182
antonymy 57–8, 182
atomism 75, 182
attributive adjective 66, 182
auto-antonyms 58, 182

B
backgrounding 128, 182
base 113, 123–4, 182
benefactive 27, 182
blended space 154, 182
blending 154, 182
bottom-up 164, 182

C
categorization 97, 99, 182
category 90, 97, 99, 182
causer 27, 182
classical 99–100, 182
Cognitive Lexical Semantics 100, 105, 115, 130–1, 173–5, 178–80, 182
Cognitive Linguistics 86–8, 182
cognitive processes 97–8, 182–3
Cognitive Semantics 88–92, 183
co-hyponyms 62, 183
colligation 66, 183
collocability 65, 183
collocation 65, 183
co-meronyms 63, 183
compatibility 65, 177, 183
complex word 5, 183
Componential Analysis 35, 75–7, 183
compound 5, 183
concept 6, 183

conceptual content 91, 120, 183
conceptual mapping 133–4, 183
Conceptual Semantics 79–80, 183
conceptual structure 91–2, 130, 183
conceptual system 92, 183
conceptualization 90, 97, 183
configuration 97, 109, 183
connotation 15, 17–18, 183
connotative 20–1, 183
construal 91, 97, 120–1, 183
context 9, 14, 184
contextual meaning 14, 164, 184
contradictory 57, 184
contrary 57, 184
conventional expressions 145–6, 164, 184
converse antonyms 58, 184

D
decompositional 74, 184
denotation 15, 17, 184
denotative 20–1, 184
descriptive meaning 19–20, 23, 184
diachronic lexicology 9, 184
dictionary theory 110, 184
dictionary view 54, 92, 184
dynamic 165, 170, 180, 184
dysphemism 22, 184

E
embodied 87, 89, 103, 184
encyclopaedic theory 6, 82, 89–90, 92, 184
encyclopaedic view 6, 82, 89–90, 92, 184
euphemism 22, 184
experiencer 27, 184
expressive meaning 19–21, 184
extension 41, 184
extra-linguistic context 14, 184

F
figurative 135–6, 146, 155, 184–5
figure 113, 128, 185
focus 127, 185
focusing 127–8, 185
foregrounding 128, 185
form 5, 185
formalist 74, 185
frame 91, 97, 112, 185
Frame semantics 109–13, 185

G
Generative Lexical Semantics 73–5, 185
goal 27, 185
gradable antonyms 57, 185
grammatical meaning 7, 11, 13–14, 25, 185
ground 113, 128, 185

H
holism 75, 185
holistic 75, 180, 185
holonym 63, 185
homography 60, 185
homonymy 60, 185
homophony 59–60, 185
hypernym 62, 185
hyponym 62, 185
hyponymy 62, 185

I
idiom 67, 186
idiomaticity 67, 186
immediate scope 127–8, 186
indeterminacy 8, 186
input spaces 154, 186
instrument 27, 186
integration 153–5, 186
intension 41, 186
interspeaker variation 167–8, 186
intraspeaker variation 167–8, 186

J
juxtaposition 63, 186

L
language 3, 87, 186
lexical field 53–5, 68, 186
lexical hierarchy 62, 186
lexical item 5, 9, 186
lexical meaning 13–14, 186
lexical relationship 109, 186
Lexical Semantics 5–6, 186
lexicology 8–9, 186
lexicon 8–9, 186
linguistic context 14, 186
linguistics 4, 186
literal meaning 14, 40, 186
location 27, 186

M
matrix 113, 186
maximal scope 127, 186
maximalist 164, 186
meaning 5–6, 173, 187
meronym 63, 187
meronymy 62–3, 187
metaphor 136–7, 187
metonymy 146–7, 187
modular/modularity 87, 187
monosemy 59, 187
morphology 3–4, 187

N
Natural Semantic Metalanguage 35, 77–8, 187
non-figurative 135, 187
non-gradable antonyms 57, 187
non-modular/non-modularity 86, 187
non-reductionist 164, 187
non-reversible lexical pair 32–3, 187

O
objectivism 92, 187
objectivist 74, 129, 187
objectivity 126, 187

P
pairing 5, 187
paradigmatic relationship 52, 56–7, 187
partonymy 62, 188
patient 26, 188
periphery 100, 174, 188
perspective 125, 188
phonetics 3, 188

phonology 3, 188
pleonasm 64, 188
polyseme 59, 188
polysemy 59, 188
possessor 27, 188
pragmatics 4, 188
predicative adjective 66, 188
prescriptivism 39, 188
primes/primitives 77, 188
profile 113, 124, 188
profiling 123–4, 188
prominence 123, 188
proposition 81, 188
prototype 100, 188

R
reference 15–16, 23, 41–2, 188
referent 42, 188
referential 46, 74, 188
relational 52–3, 188
relational antonyms 58, 188
representational 92, 188
reversible lexical pair 31, 188
reversive antonyms 58, 188

S
schematicity 122–3, 188–9
scope 113, 127–8, 189
selection restrictions 64, 189
semantic components 75, 189
semantic prosody 65, 189
semantic roles 26, 189
semantic structure 92, 189
semantics 4, 189
sense 16, 189
sense relation 55, 189
simple word 5, 189
social meaning 21, 189
source 27, 136, 189
specificity 122–3, 189
Structural Lexical Semantics 51, 189

subjectivism 102, 189
subjectivist 92, 131, 189
subjectivity 126, 189
subordinate 62, 189
substance 166, 189
substitution 57, 190
superordinate 62, 190
symbolic 87, 190
synchronic/modern lexicology 9, 190
synonymy 60, 190
syntagmatic relation 63, 190
syntax 4, 190

T
target 136, 190
taxonomy 62, 190
theme 27, 190
time 27, 190
Traditional Lexical Semantics 39–41, 190
truth conditions 44–5, 190
truth-conditional 46, 190

U
unconventional expressions 145–6, 190
usage 165, 190
usage-based 87, 190
usage events 165, 190
use 5, 190
utterance 14, 165, 190

V
vagueness 8, 190
vantage point 125, 190

W
word 5, 190
word order 28–9, 190

Z
zeugma 64, 190